History & Geography 1000

Teacher's Guide

CONTENTS

Author: **Alpha Omega Publications**
Editor: Alan Christopherson, M.S.

Alpha Omega Publications®
804 N. 2nd Ave. E., Rock Rapids, IA 51246-1759

CURRICULUM

OVERVIEW

HISTORY & GEOGRAPHY

Curriculum Overview
Grades 1–12

History & Geography LIFEPAC Overview

	Grade 1	Grade 2	Grade 3
LIFEPAC 1	I AM A SPECIAL PERSON • God made me • You are God's child • All about you • Using proper manners	FAMILIES AND NEIGHBORS • We need a family • We help our family • Our neighborhood • Helping our neighbors	FISHING IN MAINE • At look at Deer Island • A lobster boat • Planting lobster traps • Catching lobsters
LIFEPAC 2	COMMUNICATING WITH SOUND • Sounds people make • Sounds that communicate • Communicating without sound • Communicating with God	COMMUNITY HELPERS • What is a community • Community helpers • Your church community • Helping your community	FARMING IN KANSAS • The six parts of Kansas • Getting to know Kansas • Exploring Kansas • Harvest in Kansas
LIFEPAC 3	I HAVE FEELINGS • I feel sad • I feel afraid • I feel happy • I have other feelings	NEIGHBORHOOD STORES • Pioneer goods and services • Modern goods and services • Some business rules • God's business rules	FRUIT-GROWING IN WASHINGTON • Geography of Washington • Cities in Washington • Apple blossom time • Apple harvest time
LIFEPAC 4	I LIVE IN A FAMILY • My mother and father • My brothers and sisters • My grandparents • What my family does	FARMS AND CITIES • Farming long ago • Farming today • Growing cities • Changing cities	FORESTS IN OREGON • A land of forests • Trees of the forests • Lumbering in Oregon • Keeping Oregon's forests
LIFEPAC 5	YOU AND GOD'S FAMILY • Getting ready in the morning • Walking to school • The school family • The church family	NEIGHBORS AROUND THE WORLD • Things all families need • How communities share • How communities change • Customs of the world	CALIFORNIA: A GOLDEN LAND • Early California • The ranch community • A trip around the state • Work on a truck farm
LIFEPAC 6	PLACES PEOPLE LIVE • Life on the farm • Life in the city • Life by the sea	A JAPANESE FAMILY • Places people live in Japan • School in Japan • Work in Japan • Play in Japan	CATTLE IN TEXAS • Learning about Texas • Early ranches in Texas • Life on a ranch • A cattle round-up
LIFEPAC 7	COMMUNITY HELPERS • Firemen and policemen • Doctors • City workers • Teachers and ministers	HOW WE TRAVEL • Travel in Bible times • Travel in the past • Travel today • Changes in today's world	COAL MINING IN PENNSYLVANIA • The formation of coal • Products from coal • Methods of mining coal • The state of Pennsylvania
LIFEPAC 8	I LOVE MY COUNTRY • America discovered • The Pilgrims • The United States begin • Respect for your country	MESSAGES FROM FAR AND NEAR • Communication in Bible times • Communication today • Reasons for communication • Communication without sound	MANUFACTURING IN MICHIGAN • Facts about Michigan • Interesting people of Michigan • Places in Michigan • The treasures in Michigan
LIFEPAC 9	I LIVE IN THE WORLD • The globe • Countries • Friends in Mexico • Friends in Japan	CARING FOR OUR NEIGHBORHOODS • God's plan for nature • Sin changed nature • Problems in our neighborhoods • Helping our neighborhoods	SPACE TRAVEL IN FLORIDA • A place to launch spacecraft • Worker at the Space Center • The first flights • The trip to the moon
LIFEPAC 10	THE WORLD AND YOU • You are special • Your family • Your school and church • Your world	PEOPLE DEPEND ON EACH OTHER • Depending on our families • Depending on our neighbors • Depending on our communities • Communicating with God	REVIEW OF NINE STATES • California and Kansas • Washington and Maine • Oregon and Pennsylvania • Texas, Florida, and Michigan

LIFEPAC	Grade 4	Grade 5	Grade 6
LIFEPAC 1	OUR EARTH • The surface of the earth • Early explorations of the earth • Exploring from space • Exploring the oceans	A NEW WORLD • Exploration of America • The first colonies • Conflict with Britain • Birth of the United States	WORLD GEOGRAPHY • Latitude and longitude • Western and eastern hemispheres • The southern hemisphere • Political and cultural regions
LIFEPAC 2	SEAPORT CITIES • Sydney • Hong Kong • Istanbul • London	A NEW NATION • War for Independence • Life in America • A new form of government • The Nation's early years	THE CRADLE OF CIVILIZATION • Mesopotamia • The land of Israel • The Nation of Israel • Egypt
LIFEPAC 3	DESERT LANDS • What is a desert? • Where are the deserts? • How do people live in the desert?	A TIME OF TESTING • Louisiana Purchase • War of 1812 • Sectionalism • Improvements in trade & travel	GREECE AND ROME • Geography of the region • Beginning civilizations • Contributions to other civilizations • The influence of Christianity
LIFEPAC 4	GRASSLANDS • Grasslands of the world • Ukraine • Kenya • Argentina	A GROWING NATION • Andrew Jackson's influence • Texas & Oregon • Mexican War • The Nation divides	THE MIDDLE AGES • The feudal system • Books and schools • The Crusades • Trade and architecture
LIFEPAC 5	TROPICAL RAIN FORESTS • Facts about rain forests • Rain forests of the world • The Amazon rain forest • The Congo rain forest	A DIVIDED NATION • Civil War • Reconstruction • Gilded Age • The need for reform	SIX SOUTH AMERICAN COUNTRIES • Brazil • Colombia • Venezuela • Three Guianas
LIFEPAC 6	THE POLAR REGIONS • The polar regions: coldest places in the world • The Arctic polar region • The Antarctic polar region	A CHANGING NATION • Progressive reforms • Spanish-American War • World War I • Roaring Twenties	OTHER AMERICAN COUNTRIES • Ecuador and Peru • Bolivia and Uruguay • Paraguay and Argentina • Chile
LIFEPAC 7	MOUNTAIN COUNTRIES • Peru – the Andes • The Incas and modern Peru • Nepal – the Himalayas • Switzerland – the Alps	DEPRESSION AND WAR • The Great Depression • War begins in Europe • War in Europe • War in the Pacific	AFRICA • Geography and cultures • Countries of northern Africa • Countries of central Africa • Countries of southern Africa
LIFEPAC 8	ISLAND COUNTRIES • Islands of the earth • Cuba • Iceland • Japan	COLD WAR • Korean War & other crises • Vietnam War • Civil Rights Movement • Upheaval in America	MODERN WESTERN EUROPE • The Renaissance • The Industrial Revolution • World War I • World War II
LIFEPAC 9	NORTH AMERICA • Geography • Lands, lakes and rivers • Northern countries • Southern countries	THE END OF THE MILLENNIUM • Watergate and Détente • The fall of Communism • Persian Gulf War • Issues of the new millennium	MODERN EASTERN EUROPE • Early government • Early churches • Early countries • Modern countries
LIFEPAC 10	OUR WORLD IN REVIEW • Europe and the explorers • Asia and Africa • Southern continents • North America, North Pole	THE UNITED STATES OF AMERICA • Beginning America until 1830 • Stronger America 1830-1930 • 1930 to the end of the Millennium • The new Millennium	THE DEVELOPMENT OF OUR WORLD • Cradle of civilization • The Middle Ages • Modern Europe • South America and Africa

History & Geography LIFEPAC Overview

	Grade 7	Grade 8	Grade 9
LIFEPAC 1	WHAT IS HISTORY • Definition of history • Characteristics of historians • The historical method • Views of history	EUROPE COMES TO AMERICA • Voyages of Columbus • Spanish exploration • Other exploration • The first colonies	UNITED STATES HERITAGE • American colonies • Acquisitions and annexations • Backgrounds to freedom • Backgrounds to society
LIFEPAC 2	WHAT IS GEOGRAPHY • Classes of geography • Relief of the earth • Types of maps • Time zones	BRITISH AMERICA • English colonies • Government • Lifestyle • Wars with France	OUR NATIONAL GOVERNMENT • Ideals of national government • National government developed • Legislative and Executive branches • Judicial branch
LIFEPAC 3	ANTHROPOLOGY • Understanding anthropology • The unity of man • The diversity of man • The culture of man	THE AMERICAN REVOLUTION • British control • Rebellion of the Colonies • War for independence • Constitution	STATE AND LOCAL GOVERNMENT • Powers of state government • County government • Township government • City government
LIFEPAC 4	SOCIOLOGY • Sociology defined • Historical development • Importance to Christians • Method of sociology	A FIRM FOUNDATION • Washington's presidency • Adams administration • Jeffersonian Democracy • War of 1812	PLANNING A CAREER • Definition of a career • God's will concerning a career • Selecting a career • Preparation for a career
LIFEPAC 5	ECONOMICS • Economics defined • Methods of the economist • Tools of the economist • An experiment in economy	A GROWING NATION • Jacksonian Era • Northern border • Southern border • Industrial Revolution	CITIZENSHIP • Citizenship defined • Gaining citizenship • Rights of citizenship • Responsibilities of citizenship
LIFEPAC 6	POLITICAL SCIENCE • Definition of political science • Roots of Western thought • Modern political thinkers • Political theory	THE CIVIL WAR • Division & Secession • Civil War • Death of Lincoln • Reconstruction	THE EARTH AND MAN • Man inhabits the earth • Man's home on the earth • Man develops the earth • The future of the earth
LIFEPAC 7	U.S. HISTORY AND GEOGRAPHY • Geography of the U.S. • Early history of the U.S. • Physical regions of the U.S. • Cultural regions of the U.S.	GILDED AGE TO PROGRESSIVE ERA • Rise of industry • Wild West • America as a world power • Progressive era	REGIONS OF THE WORLD • A region defined • Geographic and climate regions • Cultural and political regions • Economic regions of Europe
LIFEPAC 8	U.S. ANTHROPOLOGY • Native Americans • Immigrants from Europe • Other immigrants • A melting pot	A WORLD IN CONFLICT • World War I • Great Depression • New Deal • World War II	MAN AND HIS ENVIRONMENT • The physical environment • Drug abuse • The social environment • Man's responsibilities
LIFEPAC 9	STATE ECONOMICS AND POLITICS • Background of state government • State government • State finance • State politics	COLD WAR AMERICA • Origins of the Cold War • Vietnam • Truman to Nixon • Ending of the Cold War	TOOLS OF THE GEOGRAPHER • The globe • Types of maps • Reading maps • The earth in symbol form
LIFEPAC 10	SOCIAL SCIENCES REVIEW • History and geography • Anthropology • Sociology • Economics and politics	UNITED STATES REVIEW • Europe to independence • Colonies to the Civil War • Civil War to World War II • World War II through Cold War	MAN IN A CHANGING WORLD • Development of the nation • Development of government • Development of the earth • Solving problems

	Grade 10	Grade 11	Grade 12
LIFEPAC 1	ANCIENT CIVILIZATION • Origin of civilization • Early Egypt • Assyria and Babylonia • Persian civilization	FOUNDATIONS OF DEMOCRACY • Democracy develops • Virginia • New England colonies • Middle and southern colonies	INTERNATIONAL GOVERNMENTS • Why have governments • Types of governments • Governments in our world • Political thinkers
LIFEPAC 2	ANCIENT CIVILIZATIONS • India • China • Greek civilization • Roman Empire	CONSTITUTIONAL GOVERNMENT • Relations with England • The Revolutionary War • Articles of Confederation • Constitution of the U.S.	UNITED STATES GOVERNMENT • U.S. Constitution • Bill of Rights • Three branches of government • Legislative process
LIFEPAC 3	THE MEDIEVAL WORLD • Early Middle Ages • Middle Ages in transition • High Middle Ages	NATIONAL EXPANSION • A strong federal government • Revolution of 1800 • War of 1812 • Nationalism and sectionalism	AMERICAN PARTY SYSTEM • American party system • Development political parties • Functions of political parties • Voting
LIFEPAC 4	RENAISSANCE AND REFORMATION • Changes in government and art • Changes in literature and thought • Advances in science • Reform within the Church	A NATION DIVIDED • Issues of division • Division of land and people • Economics of slavery • Politics of slavery	HISTORY OF GOVERNMENTS • Primitive governments • Beginnings of Democracy • Feudalism, Theocracy & Democracy • Fascism & Nazism
LIFEPAC 5	GROWTH OF WORLD EMPIRES • England and France • Portugal and Spain • Austria and Germany • Italy and the Ottoman Empire	A NATION UNITED AGAIN • Regionalism • The division • The Civil War • Reconstruction	THE CHRISTIAN & GOVERNMENT • Discrimination & the Christian • Christian attitudes • "Opinion & Truth" in politics • Politics & Propaganda
LIFEPAC 6	THE AGE OF REVOLUTION • Factors leading to revolution • The English Revolution • The American Revolution • The French Revolution	INVOLVEMENT AT HOME & ABROAD • Surge of industry • The industrial lifestyle • Isolationism • Involvement in conflict	FREE ENTERPRISE • Economics • Competition • Money through history • International finance & currency
LIFEPAC 7	THE INDUSTRIAL REVOLUTION • Sparks of preparation • Industrial revolution in England • Industrial revolution in America • Social changes of the revolution	THE SEARCH FOR PEACE • The War and its aftermath • The Golden Twenties • The Great Depression • The New Deal	BUSINESS AND YOU • Running a business • Government & business • Banks & Mergers • Deregulation & Bankruptcy
LIFEPAC 8	TWO WORLD WARS • Mounting tension • World War I • Peace and power quests • World War II	A NATION AT WAR • Causes of the war • World War II • Korean Conflict • Vietnam Conflict	THE STOCK MARKET • How it started and works • Selecting stocks • Types of stocks • Tracking stocks
LIFEPAC 9	THE COLD WAR • The Cold War • Korean War and Vietnam War • Collapse of the Soviet Union • Today's world	CONTEMPORARY AMERICA • America in the 1960s • America in the 1970s • America in the 1980s & 90s • International Scene 1980-Present	BUDGET AND FINANCE • Cash, Credit & Checking • Buying a car • Grants, Loans & IRAs • Savings & E-cash
LIFEPAC 10	ANCIENT TIMES TO THE PRESENT • Ancient civilizations • Medieval times • The Renaissance • The modern world	UNITED STATES HISTORY • Basis of democracy • The 1800s • Industrialization • Current history	GEOGRAPHY AND REVIEW • Euro & International finance • U.S. Geography • The global traveler • Neighbors, Heroes & The Holy Land

LIFEPAC

MANAGEMENT

STRUCTURE OF THE LIFEPAC CURRICULUM

The LIFEPAC curriculum is conveniently structured to provide one teacher handbook containing teacher support material with answer keys and ten student worktexts for each subject at grade levels two through twelve. The worktext format of the LIFEPACs allows the student to read the textual information and complete workbook activities all in the same booklet. The easy to follow LIFEPAC numbering system lists the grade as the first number(s) and the last two digits as the number of the series. For example, the Language Arts LIFEPAC at the 6th grade level, 5th book in the series would be LAN0605.

Each LIFEPAC is divided into 3 to 5 sections and begins with an introduction or overview of the booklet as well as a series of specific learning objectives to give a purpose to the study of the LIFEPAC. The introduction and objectives are followed by a vocabulary section which may be found at the beginning of each section at the lower levels, at the beginning of the LIFEPAC in the middle grades, or in the glossary at the high school level. Vocabulary words are used to develop word recognition and should not be confused with the spelling words introduced later in the LIFEPAC. The student should learn all vocabulary words before working the LIFEPAC sections to improve comprehension, retention, and reading skills.

Each activity or written assignment has a number for easy identification, such as 1.1. The first number corresponds to the LIFEPAC section and the number to the right of the decimal is the number of the activity.

Teacher checkpoints, which are essential to maintain quality learning, are found at various locations throughout the LIFEPAC. The teacher should check: 1) neatness of work and penmanship, 2) quality of understanding (tested with a short oral quiz), 3) thoroughness of answers (complete sentences and paragraphs, correct spelling, etc.), 4) completion of activities (no blank spaces), and 5) accuracy of answers as compared to the answer key (all answers correct).

The self test questions are also number coded for easy reference. For example, 2.015 means that this is the 15th question in the self test of Section II. The first number corresponds to the LIFEPAC section, the zero indicates that it is a self test question, and the number to the right of the zero the question number.

The LIFEPAC test is packaged at the centerfold of each LIFEPAC. It should be removed and put aside before giving the booklet to the student for study.

Answer and test keys have the same numbering system as the LIFEPACs and appear at the back of this handbook. The student may be given access to the answer keys (not the test keys) under teacher supervision so that he can score his own work.

A thorough study of the Curriculum Overview by the teacher before instruction begins is essential to the success of the student. The teacher should become familiar with expected skill mastery and understand how these grade level skills fit into the overall skill development of the curriculum. The teacher should also preview the objectives that appear at the beginning of each LIFEPAC for additional preparation and planning.

TEST SCORING and GRADING

Answer keys and test keys give examples of correct answers. They convey the idea, but the student may use many ways to express a correct answer. The teacher should check for the essence of the answer, not for the exact wording. Many questions are high level and require thinking and creativity on the part of the student. Each answer should be scored based on whether or not the main idea written by the student matches the model example. "Any Order" or "Either Order" in a key indicates that no particular order is necessary to be correct.

Most self tests and LIFEPAC tests at the lower elementary levels are scored at 1 point per answer; however, the upper levels may have a point system awarding 2 to 5 points for various answers or questions. Further, the total test points will vary; they may not always equal 100 points. They may be 78, 85, 100, 105, etc.

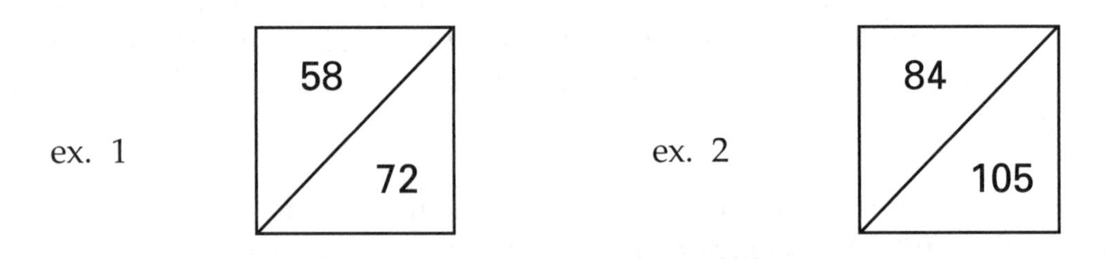

A score box similar to ex.1 above is located at the end of each self test and on the front of the LIFEPAC test. The bottom score, 72, represents the total number of points possible on the test. The upper score, 58, represents the number of points your student will need to receive an 80% or passing grade. If you wish to establish the exact percentage that your student has achieved, find the total points of his correct answers and divide it by the bottom number (in this case 72.) For example, if your student has a point total of 65, divide 65 by 72 for a grade of 90%. Referring to ex. 2, on a test with a total of 105 possible points, the student would have to receive a minimum of 84 correct points for an 80% or passing grade. If your student has received 93 points, simply divide the 93 by 105 for a percentage grade of 89%. Students who receive a score below 80% should review the LIFEPAC and retest using the appropriate Alternate Test found in the Teacher's Guide.

The following is a guideline to assign letter grades for completed LIFEPACs based on a maximum total score of 100 points.

LIFEPAC Test	=	60% of the Total Score (or percent grade)
Self Test	=	25% of the Total Score (average percent of self tests)
Reports	=	10% or 10* points per LIFEPAC
Oral Work	=	5% or 5* points per LIFEPAC

*Determined by the teacher's subjective evaluation of the student's daily work.

Example:

LIFEPAC Test Score	= 92%	92 x .60	=	55 points
Self Test Average	= 90%	90 x .25	=	23 points
Reports			=	8 points
Oral Work			=	4 points
TOTAL POINTS			=	90 points

Grade Scale based on point system:

100	–	94	=	A
93	–	86	=	B
85	–	77	=	C
76	–	70	=	D
Below		70	=	F

TEACHER HINTS and STUDYING TECHNIQUES

LIFEPAC Activities are written to check the level of understanding of the preceding text. The student may look back to the text as necessary to complete these activities; however, a student should never attempt to do the activities without reading (studying) the text first. Self tests and LIFEPAC tests are never open book tests.

Language arts activities (skill integration) often appear within other subject curriculum. The purpose is to give the student an opportunity to test his skill mastery outside of the context in which it was presented.

Writing complete answers (paragraphs) to some questions is an integral part of the LIFEPAC Curriculum in all subjects. This builds communication and organization skills, increases understanding and retention of ideas, and helps enforce good penmanship. Complete sentences should be encouraged for this type of activity. Obviously, single words or phrases do not meet the intent of the activity, since multiple lines are given for the response.

Review is essential to student success. Time invested in review where review is suggested will be time saved in correcting errors later. Self tests, unlike the section activities, are closed book. This procedure helps to identify weaknesses before they become too great to overcome. Certain objectives from self tests are cumulative and test previous sections; therefore, good preparation for a self test must include all material studied up to that testing point.

The following procedure checklist has been found to be successful in developing good study habits in the LIFEPAC curriculum.

1. Read the introduction and Table of Contents.
2. Read the objectives.
3. Recite and study the entire vocabulary (glossary) list.
4. Study each section as follows:
    a. Read the introduction and study the section objectives.
    b. Read all the text for the entire section, but answer none of the activities.
    c. Return to the beginning of the section and memorize each vocabulary word and definition.
    d. Reread the section, complete the activities, check the answers with the answer key, correct all errors, and have the teacher check.
    e. Read the self test but do not answer the questions.
    f. Go to the beginning of the first section and reread the text and answers to the activities up to the self test you have not yet done.
    g. Answer the questions to the self test without looking back.
    h. Have the self test checked by the teacher.
    i. Correct the self test and have the teacher check the corrections.
    j. Repeat steps a–i for each section.

5. Use the SQ3R* method to prepare for the LIFEPAC test.
6. Take the LIFEPAC test as a closed book test.
7. LIFEPAC tests are administered and scored under direct teacher supervision. Students who receive scores below 80% should review the LIFEPAC using the SQ3R* study method and take the Alternate Test located in the Teacher Handbook. The final test grade may be the grade on the Alternate Test or an average of the grades from the original LIFEPAC test and the Alternate Test.

   *SQ3R: **S**can the whole LIFEPAC.
   Question yourself on the objectives.
   Read the whole LIFEPAC again.
   Recite through an oral examination.
   Review weak areas.

GOAL SETTING and SCHEDULES

Each school must develop its own schedule, because no single set of procedures will fit every situation. The following is an example of a daily schedule that includes the five LIFEPAC subjects as well as time slotted for special activities.

Possible Daily Schedule

8:15	–	8:25	Pledges, prayer, songs, devotions, etc.
8:25	–	9:10	Bible
9:10	–	9:55	Language Arts
9:55	–	10:15	Recess (juice break)
10:15	–	11:00	Mathematics
11:00	–	11:45	History & Geography
11:45	–	12:30	Lunch, recess, quiet time
12:30	–	1:15	Science
1:15	–		Drill, remedial work, enrichment*

*Enrichment: Computer time, physical education, field trips, fun reading, games and puzzles, family business, hobbies, resource persons, guests, crafts, creative work, electives, music appreciation, projects.

Basically, two factors need to be considered when assigning work to a student in the LIFEPAC curriculum.

The first is time. An average of 45 minutes should be devoted to each subject, each day. Remember, this is only an average. Because of extenuating circumstances a student may spend only 15 minutes on a subject one day and the next day spend 90 minutes on the same subject.

The second factor is the number of pages to be worked in each subject. A single LIFEPAC is designed to take 3 to 4 weeks to complete. Allowing about 3-4 days for LIFEPAC introduction, review, and tests, the student has approximately 15 days to complete the LIFEPAC pages. Simply take the number of pages in the LIFEPAC, divide it by 15 and you will have the number of pages that must be completed on a daily basis to keep the student on schedule. For example, a LIFEPAC containing 45 pages will require 3 completed pages per day. Again, this is only an average. While working a 45 page LIFEPAC, the student may complete only 1 page the first day if the text has a lot of activities or reports, but go on to complete 5 pages the next day.

Long range planning requires some organization. Because the traditional school year originates in the early fall of one year and continues to late spring of the following year, a calendar should be devised that covers this period of time. Approximate beginning and completion dates can be noted on the calendar as well as special occasions such as holidays, vacations and birthdays. Since each LIFEPAC takes 3-4 weeks or eighteen days to complete, it should take about 180 school days to finish a set of ten LIFEPACs. Starting at the beginning school date, mark off eighteen school days on the calendar and that will become the targeted completion date for the first LIFEPAC. Continue marking the calendar until you have established dates for the remaining nine LIFEPACs making adjustments for previously noted holidays and vacations. If all five subjects are being used, the ten established target dates should be the same for the LIFEPACs in each subject.

FORMS

The sample weekly lesson plan and student grading sheet forms are included in this section as teacher support materials and may be duplicated at the convenience of the teacher.

The student grading sheet is provided for those who desire to follow the suggested guidelines for assignment of letter grades found on page 3 of this section. The student's self test scores should be posted as percentage grades. When the LIFEPAC is completed the teacher should average the self test grades, multiply the average by .25 and post the points in the box marked self test points. The LIFEPAC percentage grade should be multiplied by .60 and posted. Next, the teacher should award and post points for written reports and oral work. A report may be any type of written work assigned to the student whether it is a LIFEPAC or additional learning activity. Oral work includes the student's ability to respond orally to questions which may or may not be related to LIFEPAC activities or any type of oral report assigned by the teacher. The points may then be totaled and a final grade entered along with the date that the LIFEPAC was completed.

The Student Record Book which was specifically designed for use with the Alpha Omega curriculum provides space to record weekly progress for one student over a nine week period as well as a place to post self test and LIFEPAC scores. The Student Record Books are available through the current Alpha Omega catalog; however, unlike the enclosed forms these books are not for duplication and should be purchased in sets of four to cover a full academic year.

WEEKLY LESSON PLANNER

Week of:

	Subject	Subject	Subject	Subject
Monday				
	Subject	Subject	Subject	Subject
Tuesday				
	Subject	Subject	Subject	Subject
Wednesday				
	Subject	Subject	Subject	Subject
Thursday				
	Subject	Subject	Subject	Subject
Friday				

WEEKLY LESSON PLANNER

Week of:

Subject	Subject	Subject	Subject
Monday			
Subject	Subject	Subject	Subject
Tuesday			
Subject	Subject	Subject	Subject
Wednesday			
Subject	Subject	Subject	Subject
Thursday			
Subject	Subject	Subject	Subject
Friday			

Student Name ______________________ Year __________

Bible

LP #	Self Test Scores by Sections 1	2	3	4	5	Self Test Points	LIFEPAC Test	Oral Points	Report Points	Final Grade	Date
01											
02											
03											
04											
05											
06											
07											
08											
09											
10											

History & Geography

LP #	Self Test Scores by Sections 1	2	3	4	5	Self Test Points	LIFEPAC Test	Oral Points	Report Points	Final Grade	Date
01											
02											
03											
04											
05											
06											
07											
08											
09											
10											

Language Arts

LP #	Self Test Scores by Sections 1	2	3	4	5	Self Test Points	LIFEPAC Test	Oral Points	Report Points	Final Grade	Date
01											
02											
03											
04											
05											
06											
07											
08											
09											
10											

Student Name ______________________ Year ________

Mathematics

LP #	Self Test Scores by Sections 1	2	3	4	5	Self Test Points	LIFEPAC Test	Oral Points	Report Points	Final Grade	Date
01											
02											
03											
04											
05											
06											
07											
08											
09											
10											

Science

LP #	Self Test Scores by Sections 1	2	3	4	5	Self Test Points	LIFEPAC Test	Oral Points	Report Points	Final Grade	Date
01											
02											
03											
04											
05											
06											
07											
08											
09											
10											

Spelling/Electives

LP #	Self Test Scores by Sections 1	2	3	4	5	Self Test Points	LIFEPAC Test	Oral Points	Report Points	Final Grade	Date
01											
02											
03											
04											
05											
06											
07											
08											
09											
10											

TEACHER
NOTES

INSTRUCTIONS FOR HISTORY & GEOGRAPHY

The LIFEPAC curriculum from grades two through twelve is structured so that the daily instructional material is written directly into the LIFEPACs. The student is encouraged to read and follow this instructional material in order to develop independent study habits. The teacher should introduce the LIFEPAC to the student, set a required completion schedule, complete teacher checks, be available for questions regarding both content and procedures, administer and grade tests, and develop additional learning activities as desired. Teachers working with several students may schedule their time so that students are assigned to a quiet work activity when it is necessary to spend instructional time with one particular student.

The Teacher Notes section of the Teacher's Guide lists the required or suggested materials for the LIFEPACs and provides additional learning activities for the students. The materials section refers only to LIFEPAC materials and does not include materials which may be needed for the additional activities. Additional learning activities provide a change from the daily school routine, encourage the student's interest in learning, and may be used as a reward for good study habits.

I. MATERIALS NEEDED

Required:

Suggested:
encyclopedia
Bible
dictionary

II. ADDITIONAL LEARNING ACTIVITIES

Section I Meaning and Origin of Civilization

1. Construct a chart showing the non-Biblical views of man's origins on the one hand, and the Biblical views of man's origins on the other. Lead a class discussion based on material from the chart.

2. Show a movie or filmstrip about early civilization. Afterward, have a class discussion about the ideas discussed in the film.

3. Put on a class play about the Fall of Man or the Flood or both.

4. Research the symbolism connected with the colors of the rainbow, the rainbow itself, and the seasons. Give a class report on your findings.

5. Make a language chart. Show on the chart how languages gave rise to early civilizations and eventually to early nations.

Section II Early Egyptian Civilization

1. Draw or find a map of ancient Egypt. Show the boundaries in a contrasting color. Label neighboring countries. Compare the map to one of modern Egypt.

2. In class discussion, compare ancient Egypt with modern Egypt. Compare political relationships with other countries, art and literature, religion, and economy.

3. Conduct a class discussion on the developments in ancient Egypt that are still evident today. In what ways was ancient Egypt a basis for modern thinking and activity?

4. Construct a bulletin board that contains pictures from ancient Egypt and from modern Egypt.

5. Research one of the outstanding rulers of ancient Egypt. Present your findings in a report to the class.

6. Visit a museum, library, or university that has a display of ancient Egyptian artifacts or pictures of them.

Section III Assyrian and Babylonian Civilizations

1. Discuss with students the laws of Hammurabi. Compare them to modern laws and rules of conduct. Discuss the fairness of the laws and why they are considered an achievement of an ancient civilization.

2. Through a chart or discussion, compare the accomplishments of the Babylonians with the accomplishments of the Assyrians.

3. Write a group story or play about life in ancient Babylon or Assyria. Act out your play or read your story to your parents or other members of the class.

Section III Assyrian and Babylonian Civilizations (cont.)

4. Stage a class debate on the accomplishments of Babylon as opposed to those of Assyria. Which accomplishments were more significant?
5. Pretend you lived in ancient Babylon or Assyria. Describe your life as a teenager during that time.
6. Explain the role of religion in the lives of the Babylonians and Assyrians.

Section IV Persian Civilization

1. List on the chalkboard or on a chart the events that were important in the rise and the fall of ancient Persia.
2. Discuss with students the reasons the Persians had multiple gods.
3. Hold a class discussion after researching other civilizations that had many gods. What did these multiple gods provide for the people? What has caused us to believe in one God?
4. Discuss the administration of the Persian Empire in comparison to the administration and government of the United States.
5. Write a paper in which you discuss how the Persian Empire might have been prevented from its fall.
6. Trace a Persian god with its counterpart from another ancient civilization. Explain the god's importance and function in that civilization.

I. MATERIALS NEEDED

Required:

Suggested:
encyclopedia
Bible
dictionary

II. ADDITIONAL LEARNING ACTIVITIES

Section I The Far East

1. Discuss these questions with your students.

   a. What was a *dynasty* in ancient China? How are dynasties used by modern historians to trace Chinese history?

   b. How did Chinese philosophers such as Confucius differ from the thinkers of India and Greece? With what did the Chinese philosophers concern themselves?

   c. How did the *castes* of India differ from our *classes* today? How were they similar?

   d. Was ancient China governed in a similar fashion to China today? Why have we known so little until recently about the life in modern China?

2. If one is available, show a movie depicting life in India today. Point out the problems India faces, and what some of the solutions might be.

3. Visit an art gallery or museum that has displays of Chinese and Indian art. Afterward, discuss what you have seen, emphasizing the outstanding characteristics of these types of art works.

4. As a group, discuss how geographical features, such as mountains or rivers in a region, affect the way people live. How does geography affect your way of life?

5. Research the belief of *reincarnation*. Why is it still an attractive belief to some people today? Write a brief one-page report on what *reincarnation* means and how it differs from the Christian's belief in life after death.

6. Research and write a paper on some inventions from China, such as gunpowder. Be sure to point out the effects these developments have had on man's history.

Section II The Greek Civilization

1. Point out on a large map the important sites of ancient Greece such as Athens, Troy, Olympus, Macedonia, and the ancient battlefields. Point out the important places tourists can still visit to see the ruins of the Greek Empire.

2. Discuss with the students the meaning of democracy and its origins in ancient Greece.

3. Discuss with the students the fact that there are various ways to learn and several ways to teach, including the method used by Socrates. Try the Socratic method with members of your class. Discuss their reactions to it.

4. Point out that the history of Greece was in large part determined by its location on the Aegean Sea and by its rocky soil. How has location and geography influenced the history of the United States?

Section II The Greek Civilization (cont.)

5. Assemble a bulletin board of pictures of Greece: the Parthenon, Mount Olympus, and so forth. Assign students to research the subjects in the pictures and write their own captions to the pictures.

6. Write and produce a skit around one day in the lives of some Spartan youths. The skit should emphasize the harsh discipline and warlike Spartan ideals of that time and how different they were from our own.

7. Research the original Olympic games in Greece. Write a short paper comparing the early games to those held today. Which events are still held? Which games did the Greeks participate in that we no longer have?

8. Read and then write a report on a portion of one of the works of Homer, such as the *Odyssey* or the *Iliad*. Have your teacher approve your selection before you begin.

Section III The Roman Empire

1. Discuss these questions with your students.

   a. Was the history of Rome a violent one? Support your answer with examples.

   b. What was the status of women in ancient Rome? Did they have more or less rights than women today?

   c. How did God prepare the Roman Empire for the arrival of Jesus and the spread of the Gospel?

   d. In what ways was the Roman Empire and its culture similar to that of Greece?

2. Using an encyclopedia and available resources, research and prepare a report on the Roman army—its soldiers, weapons, and tactics. Tell how Rome was able to maintain military control for centuries over much of the civilized world. Report to the class.

3. Prepare a bulletin board on ancient Rome. Research and write captions for the pictures used.

4. Choose a selection from one of the Roman authors such as Virgil, Plutarch, or Tacitus. The selection need not be a long one, but have your teacher approve it before you begin. Read the selection carefully, and write a report on it to present to the class.

5. Jesus was born into a Roman world. After further research into Roman times, write a two- to three-page paper on why it was inevitable for Him to encounter opposition from the authorities. How did the teachings of Jesus vary from the laws and customs of the time?

6. List on a chalkboard or poster board the developments that led to the decline of the Roman Empire. Discuss the reason(s) each development led to the decline.

7. Discuss why the Christian church played the role it did in the first four hundred years of its history.

8. Make a shadowbox depicting a scene from the Christian Church.

9. Make a bulletin board to show scenes from the Roman Empire. Draw the pictures or cut them from magazines.

10. Research one of the people who was prominent in the early Christian church. Write a report or give an oral report to the class.

I. MATERIALS NEEDED

Required:

Suggested:
encyclopedia
dictionary

II. ADDITIONAL LEARNING ACTIVITIES

Section I The Early Middle Ages

1. On a large map identify barbarian invaders and show where they went and what occurred after their invasions.
2. Compare in a class discussion the Germanic ideas of government with the United States' ideas of government.
3. Discuss with the students the lives, characters, and personalities of the early church leaders.
4. On a large map show the Arab invasions and discuss the results with the students.
5. Discuss the existence of the Eastern Empire in the sixth century. Discuss any changes in that role.
6. See a film or filmstrip about the Early Middle Ages. Discuss any new information you learned from the film.
7. Make a large map or poster to show important events of the Early Middle Ages.
8. Research an aspect of the historical period that particularly interests you. Write a report about it, discuss the new information with the class, or give an oral report.
9. With another student, discuss the changes that occurred during the Early Middle Ages.

Section II The Middle Ages in Transition

1. Discuss the personality and character traits of Alfred the Great and Charlemagne. Discuss how their personalities and character made them great leaders.
2. On the chalkboard or a poster board list the beginning events that led to modern European countries. Be thorough so students understand these early developments.
3. Discuss the important Vikings responsible for the invasions.
4. Show how religion was a factor in the Eastern and European developments.
5. Have a class debate on one of the subjects covered in this section.
6. Have a class discussion on the role of the church during this period of history. Discuss how events might have been different if the church's influence had been different.
7. Draw a map to identify the outcome of invasions by Vikings or to show one of the following areas before and after the Middle Ages: European countries, Byzantine Empire, or Islamic Empire.
8. Write a report on the people involved in the break between the Eastern and Roman sections of the church.

9. Bring in pictures that depict the feudal system. Discuss how this system led to trade in Europe. Try to expand the concept of the feudal system by researching other sources.
10. Discuss reasons why one country may become strong and another remain weak.
11. Compare the church-state problems in the Middle Ages with church-state problems faced in our country today. Allow students to contribute their ideas about the problems.
12. Discuss in detail the reasons for the decline of the Byzantine Empire. Could the decline have been prevented?
13. Put on a play about the feudal period of history. Perhaps you could depict a day in the life of a person who lived at that time.
14. Have a class discussion on how trade affected the empires of the time.
15. Have a class debate on the subject of political power and the church. Use modern as well as ancient examples.
16. Make a booklet about one of the people from the High Middle Ages. Draw pictures to illustrate your booklet.
17. Make a shadowbox to show a typical town in the High Middle Ages.

I. MATERIALS NEEDED

Required:
reference books or encyclopedia for research (page 20)
reference books or encyclopedia for research (page 36)

Suggested:
none

II. ADDITIONAL LEARNING ACTIVITIES

Section I Renaissance

1. Construct a map with overlays to show Europe during the Renaissance and Europe today.
2. Construct a chart that includes artistic, literary, and scientific developments of the Renaissance. List those people responsible for the developments.
3. Have each student describe a specific artist, scientist, or literary figure of the Renaissance; then have other students try to identify the person.
4. Have students discuss among themselves the strengths of England, France, Spain, and the five Italian states.
5. List scientific developments of the Renaissance. Then make a corresponding list of modern items that we have as a result of those developments.
6. Make a chart or write a paper that traces the progress from feudalism to the end of the Renaissance.

Section II Reformation

1. Use maps with overlays to trace the Reformation throughout Europe and England.
2. Discuss with students characteristics of the various religions involved in the Reformation.
3. Have students write and act out a play about the Reformation and the religious wars in Europe.
4. Have students form a panel discussion about the causes and results of the religious wars in Western Europe.
5. Write a report on one of the religions involved in the Reformation.
6. Write a report or give an oral report that compares England before and after the Reformation.

I. MATERIALS NEEDED

Required:

Suggested:
maps of Europe
world globe or flat map
encyclopedias
atlas
slated globe or map on which voyages and territorial expansions can be marked
biographical dictionary
historical atlas or set of historical maps for this period
biographies of individuals mentioned in text
pictures of individuals mentioned in text

II. ADDITIONAL LEARNING ACTIVITIES

Section I England and France

1. Discuss in class the religious conflicts of James I's reign, stressing the Puritan hopes for separation of church and state and for religious freedom versus crown control of the established Church of England.
2. Study with the class the power of taxation as a political tool. Have students draw parallels to understand the differences between England (the Petition of Right), France (the Fronde), and the United States (congressional control of federal taxation).
3. Develop a class role-playing game in which representatives of the mother country and representatives of a colony discuss the effects of mercantilism. Sample questions:
   a. Should the colony be allowed to develop a cotton mill?
   b. To whom does the gold mine belong—the natives, the colonists, or the Crown?
   c. Should raw materials being produced in the colony go only to the mother country or to an open world market?
   d. Can the colonial governor overrule local laws?
4. Dramatize one or more of the following incidents:
   a. a Parliamentary debate in 1628 which led to the Petition of Right
   b. a discussion between Charles I and his ministers over "ship money"
   c. a group of Puritans in 1630 deciding whether or not to emigrate to America
   d. a French nobleman and his wife discussing life at the court of Versailles
5. Draw a large map on which the colonies of England and France are shown in contrasting colors.
6. Prepare a written or oral report on one of the following topics:
   a. Mary, Queen of Scots, mother of James I
   b. the translators who developed the King James Bible
   c. Guy Fawkes
   d. Huguenots in the New World
   e. Louis IV

Section I England and France (cont.)

7. Pretend you are a young seaman going on a voyage to the New World or on Magellan's voyage around the world. Write some imaginary letters home which tell something about daily life aboard your vessel, the personality of your famous captain, the countries seen, and other events of the voyage.

8. On a map of Europe, indicate the sites of the following events:
   a. defeat of the Spanish Armada
   b. battle of Nasby
   c. battle of Blenheim
   d. Edict of Nantes
   e. Treaty of Utrecht

Section II Portugal and Spain

1. Display and discuss pictures showing the buildings and other artifacts of the Aztec and Inca civilizations.

2. Discuss the place of the Catholic Church in the development of Latin America. Include pictures of early missions and missionaries, if possible.

3. Ask the class to summarize reasons for Spain's success as a colonial power and tell why Spain eventually lost that power.

4. Visit a museum that has examples of Aztec and Inca pottery, stone work, jewelry, and textiles.

5. Put together one issue of a newspaper which might have been published in Spain during the Colonial Period. Possible news features might be the following ones: the conquest of Peru, Cortez's meeting with Montezuma, ship arrivals and sailings, sales of imported goods, and fashion illustrations. Have some members draw illustrations.

6. Create a class mural showing a busy New World harbor or a Spanish mission in the old Southwest. Include typical persons and activities after doing research on costumes and so forth.

7. Hold a class debate on the following issue of whether the presence of Spain in the New World was more beneficial than detrimental to native people there.

8. Prepare an oral or written report on one of the following topics:
   a. Lima, Peru
   b. Henry the Navigator
   c. Martin Luther
   d. sailing ships of the sixteenth and seventeenth centuries
   e. piracy on the Spanish Main
   f. the Aztec calendar
   g. recent theories about the origins of the Aztec and Inca people

Section II Portugal and Spain (cont.)

9. Discover what you can about modern Brazil and remnants of Portuguese culture that exist there. Prepare a brief oral report.

10. Find out which countries or sections of countries in North and South America and the West Indies speak these languages today: Spanish, English, Portuguese, and French. Illustrate with a four-color map.

11. Look up and explain the following words, now commonly used in English, which are Spanish in origin. Try to add others to the list:

rodeo	arroyo	galleon
adobe	mesa	doubloon
tamale	canyon	macho

Section III Austria, Germany, Italy, and the Ottoman Empire

1. Discuss Frederick the Great as an example of the "benevolent dictator."
2. Summarize the main tenets of the Muslim faith, contrasting it with Christian belief.
3. Ask the class to supply contemporary examples of the interweaving of economics and politics, such as the impact of corn and cotton imports on the Ottoman Empire.
4. Gather and display pictures which show examples of the Italian Baroque style in architecture, sculpture, painting, decoration, theatrical design, and so forth. If possible, have class members find and perform some of the works of Baroque composers.
5. Make a products map of the world, dating 1600-1800, showing where Europe obtained cotton, silk, corn, tobacco, gold, silver, diamonds, spices, ebony, ivory, sugar, coffee, and chocolate.
6. Make a map of the world today, showing which countries are largely Muslim in religion. In a different color show countries which have large Muslim minorities.
7. Read and report on a travel article or recent book about one of the countries of *Eastern* Europe mentioned in the LIFEPAC or an area once part of the Ottoman Empire as shown on page 51 of the LIFEPAC.
8. Find a copy of the Koran and look for passages that seem to offer important rules of conduct. Contrast these with Biblical commandments.
9. Read and report on a biography of one of the historical personages in this section.
10. Read about the scientific discoveries of Copernicus and Galileo, and write a brief report on their ideas.
11. Find examples of Persian art, architecture, and literature to share with your class.

I. MATERIALS NEEDED

Required:

Suggested:
maps of Europe, Great Britain, and the United States
copies of the United States Constitution and Declaration of Independence
encyclopedias

II. ADDITIONAL LEARNING ACTIVITIES

Section I English Revolution

1. Discuss with students ideas such as struggles between Parliament and the king and their culmination under the Stuart kings.
2. Discuss with students the religious climate in England and the changes under the Stuart kings. Discuss why Parliament was careful to keep Catholics off the throne.
3. Visit a museum that has an emphasis on English history.
4. Show a film of England that shows the places mentioned in this section.
5. Write a biography of one of the English monarchs or revolutionary leaders mentioned in this section.
6. Chart the English monarchs mentioned, giving dates they reigned, measures they enacted, and a picture if possible.

Section II American Revolution

1. Make a list of the hardships of daily living facing New World settlers.
2. Make a chart showing the strengths of the American Constitution.
3. Visit any battlegrounds, museums, or historical places from the Revolutionary War period.
4. Have a class debate on American war sentiments.
5. Divide the class into groups and let each group research and report on one of the battles in the American Revolution.
6. Research the many English taxes, acts, and injustices that led Americans to revolt. List them in the order of their occurrences.
7. Research the struggle between colonies and governors for control of power in the colonies.
8. Chart the battles of the Revolutionary War on a map, listing commanders of each battle and who won.

Section III French Revolution

1. On a chart or chalkboard, list the complaints of a Third Estate Frenchman under the monarchy. Discuss these complaints with students.
2. Discuss with students what caused the riots ending in the capture of the Bastille and what actions were taken by the National Assembly for the people's betterment.
3. Show a film of France, especially one dealing with places studied in class.
4. Visit a museum that has an emphasis on French history.
5. Divide students into groups, each group researching and reporting on a battle or conflict in the French Revolution.
6. Research and report on the Reign of Terror that followed Danton's dictatorship.
7. Draw maps showing France before, during, and after the Napoleonic Era.
8. Write a biography of one of the French leaders mentioned.

I. MATERIALS NEEDED

Required:

Suggested:
encyclopedias

II. ADDITIONAL LEARNING ACTIVITIES

Section I Industrial Revolution in England

1. Discuss these questions with your students.
   a. What were factors in early European living that paved the way for the coming Industrial Revolution?
   b. What was the importance of the printing press to an English businessman?
   c. What part did stockholders play in corporations?
2. Ask students to tell how English inventions aided production and efficiency.
3. List on a chalkboard the good and bad effects of the Industrial Age.
4. Have a contest to see which group can list the most inventions and new processes developed during the English Industrial Revolution. This project will take research.
5. Trace the development of industry from the dependence upon manual labor to the reliance upon the machine.
6. Research and report on monastery life in a Benedictine order.
7. Research the feudal system in the Middle Ages.
8. Research trade in the Middle Ages.
9. Write a biography of an English inventor.
10. Research the power sources that have replaced steam power today.

Section II Industrial Revolution in the United States

1. List the many advantages America had for industry's growth.
2. List the inventions aiding agriculture and the improvements they brought.
3. List the inventions aiding America's textile industry.
4. List the inventions that aided fighting in the Civil War that were not present in the War of 1812.
5. Discuss what corporations do for America and for the average working man.
6. Have a contest to see which group can list the most inventions and new processes that increased industry's growth in America. (Research is necessary.)
7. Visit an inventor's home or workshop if one is nearby.
8. Research a corporation in your town, and give a breakdown of authority from president to factory worker.

Section II Industrial Revolution in the United States (cont.)

9. Debate the advantages and disadvantages of corporations.
10. Write a biography of one of America's inventors.
11. Draw a map and label the new canals, roads, and railroads in America.
12. Research industry's new inventions that influenced the Spanish-American War, World War I, and World War II.
13. Construct a model of one of the inventions of the Industrial Revolution.

Section III Social changes of the Industrial Revolution

1. Find pictures of tenement living. Discuss with students the desperate conditions there.
2. Compare life on the farm with life in the city from the viewpoints of a farm family and a city family.
3. Discuss the effects a laissez-faire policy had on the working person.
4. List the advantages labor unions brought to a worker in the past and now.
5. Describe the danger involved when tariffs are raised too high.
6. Discuss the importance of international cooperation in trade.
7. List the inventions that led to an increase in international trade.
8. List the communist and socialist countries of today.
9. Have a class debate on the pros and cons of labor unions.
10. Through research find the main imports and exports of the United States today.
11. Write a biography of Marx or Engels.
12. Research the early labor unions of America. What made them succeed or fail?
13. Describe Marx's idea of a utopian community.
14. Research and chart the differences between travel time in 1800 and today.

I. MATERIALS NEEDED

Required:

Suggested:
world map
encyclopedias

II. ADDITIONAL LEARNING ACTIVITIES

Section I World War I

1. List the factors leading to World War I.
2. List Bismarck's plans for securing German defense against France.
3. List the aggressive actions of Kaiser Wilhelm that alienated England and Russia and increased world tension in pre-war Europe.
4. Describe the German offensives of World War I.
5. Give the steps of the Allied drives from Chateau-Thierry to German surrender.
6. Invite World War I veterans to share their experiences with the class.
7. Show documentary films of World War I.
8. Assign battles of the war and have groups of students research and report.
9. Chart the major battles of World War I in detail.
10. Research war equipment of World War I and illustrate.

Section II Peace Returns

1. Discuss with students the effects of the publication of Wilson's Fourteen Points on wartime Europe.
2. Discuss with students why the Peace of Paris was not based on Wilson's Fourteen Points.
3. Describe post-World War I attitudes throughout the world.
4. Discuss the regrowth of totalitarian governments in Europe.
5. Discuss how Hitler and Mussolini lifted their nations from depression.
6. List the aggressive actions of Germany, Italy, and Japan.
7. Discuss why Europe's democratic nations allowed Germany to continue its aggression.
8. List the factors that led to World War II.
9. Invite people who lived during Hitler's time to talk about his influence.
10. Chart the changing boundaries in pre-World War II Europe as a class on a large map, giving dates of changes.
11. Write a biography of Hitler or Mussolini.
12. Research the terms of the Peace of Paris for each Central Power and describe the changes in Europe's map because of treaties.

Section III World War II

1. Describe the blitzkrieg strategy of Germany.
2. List the steps of the German drive for power in Europe.
3. List the steps of the Allied drive in Europe after America entered the war.
4. Describe the American offensive in the Pacific.
5. Explain why atomic bombs were dropped on Japan.
6. Discuss factors that hindered the peace settlements after World War II.
7. Explain what divided America and Russia after World War II.
8. Discuss what led nations to form the United Nations.
9. Invite World War II veterans to speak on their experiences.
10. Show films on the war or the United Nations.
11. Stage a mock United Nations General Assembly and discuss an international problem.
12. Research and chart an offensive of World War II and present it to the class.
13. On a world map chart the nations under communist control today.

I. MATERIALS NEEDED

Required:	Suggested:
	world map
	encyclopedias
	almanac

II. ADDITIONAL LEARNING ACTIVITIES

Section I The Cold War

1. Hold a summit meeting between the "leaders" of the world powers. Have students use role playing to act the parts of the Soviet Union, Great Britain, and the United States near the end of World War II. The class should discuss these items:

   a. the main issues after World War II

   b. the future of Europe

   c. the conflict between East and West

2. Have several students research General MacArthur's position in Korea and why he was moved from command. Allow them to report to the class and discuss these questions.

   a. Why was MacArthur removed?

   b. What was the major disagreement?

   c. Why did the removal of MacArthur coincide with the beginning of peace talks?

3. Make a class bulletin board showing the members and political loyalties for at least ten current world organizations.

4. Research the Persian Gulf War. Hold a class discussion on the question, "Could this war have happened before the reforms in the Soviet Union?"

5. Stage a debate on this subject: The Atom—Good or Evil for Man?

6. Research the Vietnam War. Have each student decide how he would have handled the crisis/war if he or she had been president. Let the students defend their positions in a class debate.

7. Lead a discussion of America's role in the Bay of Pigs invasion. Did America act wisely? What should America have done? What controversy has been sparked by the Bay of Pigs and our involvement there?

8. Research American support of a dictatorial regime during the Cold War. Possible topics: Iran, El Salvador, South Africa, Nicaragua, or any other appropriate nation. Discuss the moral implications.

Section II The World Today

1. Check a current newspaper for references to international organizations such as NATO, EC, OPEC, and OAU.

2. Do a report on the Iranian Revolution and the effect it has had on the Middle East.

3. Do a survey of the changes in the governments of Africa since the end of the Cold War. Formulate a summary of the pattern and discuss possible reasons.

4. Have the students do a profile of a military coup in a country. Discuss possible reasons why they are uncommon in western democracies.
5. Debate the following issues:
   a. Communism—is it dead or dormant?
   b. The former Soviet Union—will it become a prosperous democracy?
   c. Man's achievements—remarkable or not?
6. Most news media and journals note more disasters than achievements for mankind. Keep a log for one week of all the good and inspirational things you hear on the news or read about in the paper. Match this against a log of world disasters for the same period of time.
7. Discuss whether or not the United States should get involved if a war starts
   a. between North and South Korea,
   b. between China and Taiwan, or
   c. between Iran and Israel
8. Have the students write a paper explaining how they would create a new United Nations today. They should include how it would be organized, its powers, and its responsibilities.

I. MATERIALS NEEDED

Required:

Suggested:
encyclopedias

II. ADDITIONAL LEARNING ACTIVITIES

Section I Ancient Civilizations and Medieval Times

1. Make a chart showing significant ancient civilizations and their forms of government. Use pictures or drawings to designate the civilization and its kind of government. List or picture leaders and their major accomplishments.
2. Help students to write a play about the feudal system and the church in the Middle Ages. Help them design sets and find articles that could be used as costumes.
3. Have a group painting or drawing project in which each member is responsible for painting a part of a medieval scene. Use butcher paper or large poster board. Display the art work on a wall in the classroom.
4. Perform the play about the feudal system described in number 2.
5. Research in depth one of the leaders of an ancient civilization. Write a report and submit it to your teacher or give the report to the class as an oral report.
6. Decorate the bulletin board with pictures, drawings, or articles about the ancient civilizations.

Section II Renaissance

1. Discuss modern religious conflicts that have led to confrontation or war. Compare these to the religious conflicts of ancient times.
2. Show pictures of early inventions, art works, and works of literature. Help students to identify the artists and scientists responsible for them.
3. Make a chart that shows the changes that occurred between the Middle Ages and the Renaissance. Use pictures and drawings on your chart.
4. Have each member of the group read supplementary biographical material about each of the explorers or Reformation leaders mentioned in the section. Give a report to the class about the explorers or Reformation leaders or use role-playing in costume to act out the person's life.
5. Research in depth Napoleon's life. Write a report for your teacher or the class detailing Napoleon's personality and character.
6. Make a poster that shows the major international organizations today. Detail the membership, purpose, and length of existence of each organization.

History & Geography Notes

A L T E R N A T E

Reproducible Tests
for use with the
History & Geography 1000
Teacher's Guide

Name ______________________

Match these items (each answer, 2 points).

1. ________ civilization
2. ________ commerce and trade
3. ________ theistic evolution
4. ________ "subdue" the earth
5. ________ serpent
6. ________ Sumerian King list
7. ________ the rainbow
8. ________ Tower of Babel
9. ________ Sargon
10. ________ Egypt

a. God's mandate to man
b. united human strength in rebellion against God
c. society with developed cities
d. oral Mesopotamian account of the flood
e. conquered Sumer
f. belief that God started the evolutionary process
g. "gift of the Nile"
h. early writing
i. mark of an advanced society
j. "perpetual and everlasting" covenant
k. deceived Eve

Answer *true* or *false* (each answer, 1 point).

11. ______________ Egyptian history is divided into two main parts, the Old Kingdom and the Empire.
12. ______________ The only significant Egyptian leader after the Nineteenth Dynasty was Ramses III.
13. ______________ The ruler Menes united Egypt's diverse groups and established a capital at Memphis.
14. ______________ Sheshoq I pursued a foreign policy of alliance with Ahab of Israel.
15. ______________ The Egyptian economy was primarily agricultural.
16. ______________ Egyptian society was divided into four classes.
17. ______________ The oldest form of Egyptian writing was cuneiform.
18. ______________ Egyptian art is characterized by lack of perspective.
19. ______________ Egyptian religion was polytheistic.
20. ______________ The Babylonian Empire was composed of Mesopotamia and the lands of ancient Sumer.

Write the letter for the correct answer on each line (each answer, 2 points).

21. The ruler who saw himself as the upholder of the oppressed, common people was __________.
    a. Mursili I
    b. Nimrod
    c. Hammurabi
    d. Samsi-Adad I

22. Hammurabi is noted for his ________.
    a. code of 282 laws
    b. Mosaic Law
    c. contribution to the fall of Babylon
    d. writing of the Amarna Letters

23. The Babylonians made significant contributions in________.
    a. art and literature
    b. mathematics and astronomy
    c. social sciences
    d. the alphabet

24. The Tigris-Euphrates valley, the Fertile Crescent, and Palestine were controlled by__________.
    a. Babylon
    b. Egypt
    c. Assyria
    d. the Hittite Empire

25. When Assyria fell,_________emerged in its place.
    a. Babylon
    b. Israel
    c. Egypt
    d. Neo-Babylon

26. The chief god of the Assyrian pantheon was_________.
    a. Ishtar
    b. Ashur
    c. Nineveh
    d. Nabu

27. Most Assyrian literature was _________.
    a. written on papyrus
    b. repeated by word of mouth
    c. composed of government documents
    d. religious in nature

28. Persia was defeated by _________.
    a. Artaxerxes
    b. Cambyses II
    c. Alexander the Great
    d. Zerubbabel

29. Persian history began with the _________.
    a. Medes
    b. Persians
    c. Lydians
    d. Egyptians

30. The twenty-one Persian provinces were called _________.
    a. states
    b. mini-nations
    c. satrapies
    d. city-states

Complete these statements (each answer, 3 points).

31. The philosopher who taught the Persians a morality system based on "Do good, hate evil" was ____.

32. Early Persians worshiped gods of a. ________________________, b. ________________________, and c. ________________________.

33. In the history of Israel, the period in which Judeans were returned to their lands was known as the ____.

34. The man who interpreted Belshazzar's dream was ____.

35. The chief literary accomplishment of the neo-Babylonians was the ________________________, which catalogued their military successes.

36. The kings of Assyria portrayed artistically the histories of their campaigns by using ____.

37. Assyrian writing was a kind of script called ____.

38. One accomplishment of the Babylonians was a ________________________ calendar to aid in agriculture.

39. The oldest form of Egyptian writing was ____.

40. The classes in Egyptian society were the a. ______________________________,
b. ____________________, and c. ____________________.

41. The Egyptians believed their bodies were indwelt by a double, or ____________________, that lived after the body died.

42. The last event of God's week of Creation was the ____________________________.

78 / 98

Score ______
Teacher check ____________
Initial Date

History & Geography 1002 Alternate Test

Name ______________________________

Match these items (each answer, 2 points).

1. ________ rajah
2. ________ Himalayas
3. ________ Alexander the Great
4. ________ Great Wall
5. ________ Sparta
6. ________ Parthenon
7. ________ Greece
8. ________ Pericles
9. ________ Buddhism
10. ________ Ceasar
11. ________ Twelve Tables
12. ________ Zeus
13. ________ A.D. 325

a. protected China
b. mountains on India's borders
c. warlike and disciplined society
d. counsel of Nicaea
e. birthplace of democracy
f. spread Greek culture through conquest
g. great Athenian leader
h. collecton of Roman laws
i. famous Greek temple
j. crossed the Alps with elephants
k. contained *Four Noble Truths*
l. chief Greek god
m. Indian ruler
n. killed by Roman Senate

Write the letter for the correct answer on each line (each answer, 2 points).

14. Athens and Sparta were Greek ________.
    a. empires
    b. colonies
    c. politicians
    d. city-states

15. The Athenian philosopher who was forced to drink poisonous hemlock because of his beliefs was ____________.
    a. Plato
    b. Socrates
    c. Demosthenes
    d. Sophocles

16. Philip of Macedon was the father of Alexander the Great and an ambitious ____________.
    a. soldier and conqueror
    b. poet
    c. merchant
    d. actor

17. The Olympic games were begun by the____________.
    a. Romans
    b. Greeks
    c. Macedonians
    d. Olympians

18. Alexander the Great is remembered as ____________.
    a. a thinker
    b. a soldier
    c. an athlete
    d. a, b, and c

19. The most famous of the Greek writers was the poet Homer, who wrote __________.
    a. the *Republic*
    b. the *Aenead*
    c. the *Iliad* and the *Odyssey*
    d. *The Rise and Fall of the Roman Empire*

20. Plato was a utopian thinker, who envisioned a__________.
    a. new religion
    b. mathematical formula
    c. master race
    d. perfect society

21. "Hellenistic" refers to the __________ world.
    a. Greek
    b. Roman
    c. Cretan
    d. Spartan

22. Romulus and Remus were__________.
    a. opposing Roman generals
    b. two brothers said to have founded Rome
    c. Roman mathematicians
    d. two rulers

23. Plebeians in Rome were members of the__________.
    a. army
    b. lower classes
    c. upper classes
    d. senate

Complete these statements (each answer, 3 points).

24. Plebeians in Rome were able to negotiate more effectively for their rights when Rome's wars required greater numbers of __________________________.

25. A famous Carthaginian general who crossed the Alps into Italy during the Second Punic War was __________________________.

26. The Roman dictator who was killed in the Senate on the Ides of March in 44 B.C. was __________________________.

27. The Twelve Tables of Rome were a written set of __________________________.

28. Historians have divided the history of Rome into three parts: pre–Republic, Republic, and __________________________.

29. Free food and free entertainment for the masses in Rome were considered wrong by many citizens, who referred to the dole system as "bread and __________________________."

30. The Roman Empire rose from the ruins of, and borrowed much of its culture from, the __________________________ Empire.

31. The Roman emperor who probably set fire to Rome was __________________________.

32. The most significant event of the Roman period was the life and death of __________________.

33. Jesus offered himself as a Messiah to the __________________________.

34. Diocletian appointed ______________________ as ruler of the Western Empire.

Answer *true* or *false* (each answer, 1 point).

35. ______________ The early history of the Greek people took place on the Aegean Sea.

36. ______________ India is a land of many rivers.

37. ______________ The ancient Indian language was known as *Vedas*.

38. ______________ Chinese civilization was influenced by the fact that China had no major rivers.

39. ______________ Pure scholarship in China developed under the Han dynasty.

40. ______________ The Persians suffered a humiliating defeat at the hands of the Athenians during the Persian wars at the Battle of Marathon.

41. ____________ Persia was the birthplace of democracy.
42. ____________ The Acropolis in Athens was a temple to the goddess Athena.
43. ____________ Citizens of ancient Athens ignored the theater while they pursued other forms of art more important to them.
44. ____________ Athletics were important to ancient Greeks.
45. ____________ The Roman who married the queen of Egypt and later committed suicide was Mark Antony.
46. ____________ Unlike other states of its time, Rome treated most of the peoples it conquered fairly.
47. ____________ Diocletian made laws to prevent landowners from leaving their property.
48. ____________ St. Basil established the first monasteries in the East.

Answer these questions (each answer, 4 points).

49. Which ancient civilization devised a caste system to preserve racial purity?

____

50. Why were the Chinese philosophers considered "social" rather than "metaphysical"?

____

____

____

____

51. Why was Caesar assassinated?

____

____

____

____

52. Which of the Apostles of Jesus carried the Gospel throughout Asia Minor and as far as Greece and Rome?____

53. Who betrayed Jesus Christ?

____

81/102

Score ______

Teacher check ______
Initial Date

Name ______________________________

Match these items (each answer, 3 points).

1. __________ Attila
2. __________ Jerome
3. __________ Benedict
4. __________ Muhammad
5. __________ Charlemagne
6. __________ Genghis Khan
7. __________ Alfred the Great
8. __________ Emperor Leo III

a. "The Scourge of God
b. hermit whose rule was based on work and prayer; followers took vows of poverty, chastity and obedience
c. united Mongolian tribes; brilliant military leader
d. monk who translated the Bible into Latin.
e. leader of iconoclast movement
f. Saxon king of Wessix (A.D. 871-A.D. 899)
g. his reign was a time of culture and learning
h. messenger of Allah
i. drove Slavs from north of the Danube

Answer *true* or *false* (each answer, 2 point).

9. __________ The early Christian church was highly structured.
10. __________ In the Germanic system of law and justice, all crimes were considered disputes between individuals.
11. __________ After Justinian's death, the Germanic tribes began to take over the empire of Justinian.
12. __________ At the peak of their power, the Arabs conquered much of the Persian Empire, North Africa, and Spain.
13. __________ There is no evidence that the Vikings ever passed through Russia.
14. __________ A dynasty of strong kings resulted in a revival of the Byzantine Empire in the ninth to eleventh centuries.
15. __________ The Islamic Empire gradually became more Arabian than Persian.
16. __________ The political power of the Roman Catholic Church increased with the coronation of Charlemagne in A.D. 800.
17. __________ The economic and social system of the High Middle Ages was called feudalism.
18. __________ A fourteenth-century trade organization was the Hanseatic League.

Write the letter for the correct answer on each line (each answer, 2 points).

19. A system of government in the High Middle Ages was __________.
    a. manorialism
    b. feudalism
    c. chivalric system
    d. subinfeudation

20. One of the following events was *not* a result of growth of trade during the Middle Ages. That event was __________.
    a. money became important in Europe
    b. trade fairs were prevalent
    c. banking systems developed
    d. town populations decreased as people left to seek their fortunes.

21. A strong monarchy did not develop in Germany because __________.
    a. kings were more concerned with holding onto Italian states
    b. Germany was split into five duchies
    c. Otto dominated the nobles
    d. Frederick Barbarossa extended the empire into Asia Minor.

22. The primary reforms of the medieval church were __________.
    a. hermetic
    b. mendicant
    c. monastic
    d. papal

23. One of the reasons for the fall of the Byzantine Empire was __________.
    a. Renaissance
    b. First Crusade
    c. "Black Death"
    d. invasion of Constantinople by barbarians

24. One reason Charlemagne was an able leader was that he __________.
    a. had a carefully planned check system
    b. was feared by the common people
    c. was not supported by the Roman Church
    d. was elected king by the nobles

25. Charlemagne and Alfred the Great were noted for __________.
    a. the founding of the English kingdom
    b. the establishment of a system of roads and bridges
    c. fostering learning
    d. increasing agricultural production

26. In the tenth century the great intellectual center of Europe was __________.
    a. Aix-la-Chappelle
    b. Cordoba
    c. Rome
    d. Valencia

27. A movement by Byzantine Emperor Leo III to cover religious paintings and to destroy religious idols was called __________.
    a. scriptorium
    b. frescoes
    c. iconoclasm
    d. idolatry

28. A member of the comitatus was expected to __________.
    a. swear complete loyalty to the king in return for satisfaction of needs
    b. work in the fields and share crops with the kingsmen
    c. live in bondage for twenty years
    d. be loyal to God and swear allegiance to the state.

Answer these questions (each answer, 5 points).

29. What is the term used to describe a time of culture and learning during the reign of Charlemagne?

____

30. What were three methods of dealing with crimes under the Germanic system of law and justice?

a. ____

b. ____

c. ____

Match these items (each answer, 2 points).

31. ________ Justinian Empire
32. ________ Islam
33. ________ Holy Roman Empire
34. ________ Islamic Empire
35. ________ Bologna
36. ________ Portugal
37. ________ Carthusians
38. ________ Mongols
39. ________ Ottoman Turks
40. ________ Umayyad Kingdom

a. redivided by Treaty of Verdun
b. Mecca
c. peak reached during Abbasid dynasty
d. declared a free kingdom in 1143
e. previous Byzantine Empire
f. first formal universities were established there
g. nomadic Asiatic tribe that invaded China
h. Jewish homeland
i. center of power in Spain
j. religious reform hermits
k. Janissary corps

75 / 94

Score ______

Teacher check ______
Initial Date

History & Geography 1004 Alternate Test

Name ______________________________

Match these items (each answer, 2 points).

1. __________ Louis IX
2. __________ Flanders
3. __________ Francisco Sforza
4. __________ Leonardo da Vinci
5. __________ Petrarch
6. __________ Erasmus
7. __________ Johann Gutenberg
8. __________ John Wycliffe
9. __________ Henry VIII
10. __________ Cardinal Ximénez

a. "Father of Humanism"
b. subject of economic dispute between England and Scotland
c. printing press
d. Act of Supremacy
e. took over Duchy of Milan
f. concerned with corruption in the established church
g. responsible for first printed edition of the whole Bible in original language
h. second pope
i. Treaty of Paris
j. *The Praise of Folly*
k. *The Last Supper*

Write the letter for the correct answer on each line (each answer, 2 points).

11. The peace of Westphalia eliminated religious turmoil in Germany by ____________.
    a. declaring Catholicism to be Germany's state religion
    b. deposing Catholic King Ferdinand
    c. ensuring that Calvinists and Lutherans had the same rights
    d. setting up a court to deal with Protestant rebels

12. One reform of the Council of Trent was that ____________.
    a. it failed to affirm the Catholic doctrines
    b. clergymen were required to consider secular affairs before religious ones
    c. it lessened rules of discipline among the clergy
    d. it tended to unify the Catholic Church and to encourage the clergy

13. In 1536 a group of English peasants and some landed gentry joined a rebellion called the ____________.
    a. Pilgrimage of Grace
    b. Act of Supremacy
    c. Anglican Rebellion
    d. Peasants' Rebellion

14. John Calvin believed that____________.
    a. the Pope was the supreme head of the church
    b. dancing and gambling should be permitted among church members
    c. the Bible should be the only authority in religion
    d. Jesus Christ's presence is an actuality in the Lord's Supper

15. Isaac Newton is responsible for ____________.
    a. the assertion that the sun is the center of the universe
    b. discovering laws of gravitation and motion
    c. eyeglasses
    d. prototypes for the helicopter

16. Spanish writer Miguel de Cervantes wrote ___________.
    a. *The New Atlantis*
    b. *The Autobiography of Benvenuto Cellini*
    c. *Decameron*
    d. *Don Quixote de la Mancha*

17. Gothic architecture is characterized by ___________.
    a. thick walls and low, wide arches
    b. vaulted arches, horizontal lines, elaborate carvings, and stained glass windows
    c. complex domes and vaults atop square or rectangular structures
    d. ornate mosaics and colorful paintings

18. During the fourteenth century, the government in Florence, Italy was ___________.
    a. an oligarchy
    b. a monarchy
    c. a democracy
    d. a republic

19. The War of the Roses in England was a domestic dispute resulting from ___________.
    a. Edward II's neglect and incompetence
    b. the Archbishop's assassination
    c. King Henry VI and the Yorkist dukes both laying claim to the throne
    d. religious dissension between the Anglicans and the Catholics

20. The Tudor dynasty in England eventually brought about ___________.
    a. further wars and disagreements within England
    b. increased trade with other nations
    c. restoration of the Catholic Church in England
    d. a period of peace and prosperity

Answer *true* or *false* (each answer, 1 point).

21. ______________ Joan of Arc believed Charles VII should be crowned at Rheims.

22. ______________ The Moors were defeated in 1212 at Las Navas de Tolosa.

23. ______________ Under Ferdinand and Isabella, the Spanish Inquisition was established.

24. ______________ Giotto's paintings produced a sense of real people and real space.

25. ______________ Michelangelo was both a painter and a sculptor.

26. ______________ Boccaccio synthesized the doctrines of Christian theology and the concepts of Plato in his writings.

27. ______________ Galileo was a French scientist who is known for his discoveries in the field of astronomy.

28. ______________ Economic and political dissatisfaction among the people encouraged church reform.

29. ______________ John Huss attacked the church offices but not the sacraments.

30. ______________ Martin Luther believed that the pope could forgive sinners.

Complete these statements (each answer, 3 points).

31. The five major Italian states were a. ______________________, b. ______________________, c. ______________________, d. ______________________, and e. ______________________.

32. Three groups of religious thought in France were a. ______________________, b. ______________________, and c. ______________________.

33. In the Netherlands, the Dutch-speaking people of the northern provinces embraced the religion of a. ______________________, while the Flemish-speaking and French-speaking people of the southern provinces remained b. ______________________.

34. The Spanish Inquisition became notorious as a church court because it ______________________ ______________________.

35. In the sixteenth century in Spain, Ignatius of Loyola founded a new religious order called the ______________________, that supported Catholicism.

Match these items (each answer, 2 points).

36. __________ Ulrich Zwingli
37. __________ Conrad Grebel
38. __________ Somerset
39. __________ Edward VI
40. __________ Mary I
41. __________ Elizabeth I
42. __________ Mary Stuart
43. __________ Pope Paul IV
44. __________ Lady Jane Grey
45. __________ Robert Kett

a. became English ruler at age nine
b. index of books Catholics were not allowed to read
c. supported a religion without saints, fasting, and celibate priests
d. led 16,000 peasants in revolt in 1549
e. leader of Anabaptists in Germany, the Netherlands, and Switzerland
f. restored Protestantism in England
g. became queen upon the death of Edward VI
h. convinced Edward IV to allow him to rule the kingdom
i. claimed English throne on the grounds that Henry VIII and Anne Boleyn had never been married
j. restored Catholic religion in England
k. resigned her throne

85/106

Score __________
Teacher check __________
Initial Date

Name ______________________________

Match these items (each answer, 2 points).

1. __________ Tudors
2 __________ William III
3. __________ Treaty of Utrecht
4. __________ Guy Fawkes
5. __________ Roundhead leader
6. __________ Act of Union, 1707
7. __________ Huguenots
8. __________ Presbyterianism
9. __________ Habeas Corpus Act
10. __________ Spanish Armada
11. __________ tunnage and poundage
12. __________ Henry of Navarre
13. __________ Cavaliers
14. __________ Petition of Right
15. __________ Mazarin

a. special customs charges
b. ended the War of the Spanish Succession
c. safeguard against arbitrary imprisonment
d. king of England following the Glorious Revolution
e. predominant religion of Scotland in seventeenth century
f. French Protestants
g. despotic rulers of England
h. gave Parliament control of taxation
i. first Bourbon king of France
j. law that united Scotland and England
k. Oliver Cromwell
l. prime minister of France during reign of Louis XIV
m. plotted to blow up Parliament
n. fleet of warships
o. escaped to France
p. supporters of Charles I

Define these terms (each definition, 3 points).

16. divine right of kings ____

____

____

17. joint stock company ____

____

____

18. Encomienda ____

____

____

Match these items (each answer, 2 points).

19.	__________ Sagres	a.	conquered Peru
20.	__________ Charles V	b.	first Christian missionary to Japan.
21.	__________ Bartholomew Dias	c.	made first voyage around the world
22.	__________ Christopher Columbus	d.	Portugal's chief New World colony
23.	__________ Brazil	e.	king of the Aztecs
24.	__________ Philip II of Spain	f.	location of a Portuguese school of navigation
25.	__________ Francis Xavier	g.	Spanish king who restored Catholicism in much of Europe
26.	__________ Ferdinand Magellan	h.	explored African coast
27.	__________ Montezuma	i.	sailed west to find a route to the East Indies
		j.	sent his fleet to attack England

Write the letter for the correct answer on each line (each answer, 2 points).

28. After the Renaissance, the only Italian city-state that retained its independence was ____________.
    a. Florence
    b. Venice
    c. Milan
    d. Rome

29. English colonies in the New World were successful because ____________.
    a. religious dissenters were allowed to settle there
    b. some degree of self-government was allowed
    c. a large number of English people were willing to become colonists
    d. a, b, and c

30. Mercantilism was an economic policy that ____________.
    a. included government action to stimulate trade and promote the country's self-sufficiency
    b. was based on religious belief
    c. promoted the colonies at the expense of the mother country
    d. had nothing to do with international trade

31. The citizens of Spanish descent born in the New World were called ____________.
    a. mulattos
    b. mestizos
    c. Creoles
    d. Mexicans

32. Spain's power in the New World declined because ____________.
    a. strong leadership was lacking
    b. expensive wars drained away the riches brought from the colonies
    c. there was much corruption among civil workers
    d. a, b, and c

33. Austria played a significant role in European history by ____________.
    a. having many costly wars
    b. halting Turkish expansion into Europe
    c. being a Catholic country
    d. having extensive colonies in the New World

34. Frederick II, called Frederick the Great, increased Prussia's power by ____________.
    a. seeking powerful allies
    b. developing a democratic form of government
    c. developing a strong military force
    d. pursuing a pacifist policy

35. Defeat in battle was particularly hard for the Muslim armies to accept because they ____________.
    a. knew they had superior weapons
    b. were not really used to fighting
    c. preferred a negotiation to open warfare
    d. believed victory in battle came through divine favor

36. The Ottoman Empire lost its effectiveness because it could not ____________.
    a. adapt to rapid changes in economic conditions
    b. find a strong man to serve as leader
    c. support large armies
    d. reconcile religious belief with territorial growth

Complete these statements (each answer, 3 points).

37. A conquered city that became the capital of the Ottoman Empire was ____________________.

38. The Ottoman Empire's economy was hurt by the importation of corn and cotton from ____________________.

39. One of the principles of mercantilism was that colonies should not be allowed to produce any ____________________ that the mother country produced.

40. Under Louis XIV and his ministers, France charged low tariffs on imported ________________.

41. Education of the native people in lands conquered by Spain was in the hands of the ____________________.

Answer *true* or *false* (each answer, 1 point).

42. ______________ The Ottoman Turks conquered the Balkan states in the fourteenth century.

43. ______________ In Latin America, Spain established a social system that gave equality to all social classes.

44. ______________ Muslim leaders were eventually forced to raise armies of slaves.

45. ______________ Charles II was a sober and serious man known as the "Weeping Monarch."

46. ______________ The fur trade was important in the development of French colonies.

47. ______________ Prussia was a militaristic state with a large army.

48. ______________ Charles I escaped to France before he could be beheaded.

78 / 97

Score ______

Teacher check ____________ Initial Date

History & Geography 1006 Alternate Test

Name ______________________________

Match these items (each answer, 2 points).

1. __________ Congress
2. __________ coup d'etat
3. __________ nationalism
4. __________ Parliament
5. __________ mercantilism
6. __________ proprietor
7. __________ monarchy
8. __________ commonwealth
9. __________ divine right
10. __________ Tory

a. devotion to one's country
b. English lawmaking body
c. total rule by a sovereign
d. God's will to rule
e. person with exclusive right to rule a colony
f. sudden siezure of government
g. one who seeks power for the Parliament
h. America's lawmaking body
i. government in which people are sovereign
j. support of mother country by her colonies
k. a supporter of the king's power

Write the letter for the correct answer on each line (each answer, 3 points).

11. English political parties favoring a strong Parliament were the a. ____________________ and the b. ____________________.
12. The English Revolution ended the long struggle for power between the a. ________________ and the b. ____________________.
13. The houses of Parliament are the a. ____________________ and b. ____________________.
14. The houses of Congress are the a. ____________________ and b. ____________________.
15. American colonies were founded by a. ____________________ or b. ____________________.
16. The value of the French and Indian War to America was ______________________________ ____.
17. Legislative bodies during the French Revolution included the National Assembly, a. ____________________, and b. ____________________.
18. After ruling as a. ____________________, Napoleon declared himself French b. ____________________ in 1804.
19. Napoleon made reforms in France's banking, a. ____________________, and b. ____________________.
20. Events leading to Napoleon's fall started with his invasion of ____________________.

Briefly explain the significance of each of the following items (each answer, 3 points).

21. growing power of Parliament ______________________________

____

22. Declaration of Independence ______________________________

____

23. battle of Yorktown ______________________________

____

24. Declaration of the Rights of Man ______________________________

____

25. battle of Nations ______________________________

____

26. battle of Waterloo ______________________________

____

Underline the answer that does *not* fit (each answer, 3 points).

27. Factors increasing Parliament's power were these:

    a. kings caring little about domestic affairs
    b. Bill of Rights
    c. English Revolution
    d. Pride's Purge

28. English measures which infuriated American colonists included these actions:

    a. English Trade Acts
    b. blockade of New York
    c. unfair taxing
    d. trials without juries

29. Factors leading to Napoleon's takeover of France included these:

    a. rise as a national hero
    b. confusion of French life
    c. loss to Syria
    d. military genius

30. All three revolutions—English, American, and French—gave to their people these freedoms:

    a. new personal rights and freedoms
    b. more voice in government
    c. freedom from king's rule
    d. greater equality

83 / 104

Score ______

Teacher check ______________
Initial Date

Name ______________________________

Match these items (each answer, 3 points).

1.	__________ Fulton	a.	steel plow
2.	__________ Stephenson	b.	*Communist Manifesto*
3.	__________ Oliver	c.	Rocket
4.	__________ Marx	d.	reaping machine
5.	__________ Cooper	e.	standardized parts
6.	__________ Whitney	f.	road improvement
7.	__________ McAdam	g.	spinning jenny
8.	__________ Smith	h.	*Clermont*
9.	__________ Watt	i.	steam engine
10.	__________ Hargreaves	j.	*Tom Thumb*
		k.	laissez-faire

Complete these statements (each answer, 4 points).

11. The world-wide change from hand labor to machines is called the ______________________ Revolution.
12. The overthrow of capitalism by the working class is sought by ______________________.
13. *Proletariat* is another term for the ______________________.
14. *Bourgeoisie* is another term for the ______________________.
15. The mass movement from the country to the city is called ______________________.
16. Negotiations with employers by labor leaders is called ______________________.
17. The development of mass improvements for farmers was called the ______________________ ______________________.
18. The policy opposing government intervention in economics is called ______________________.
19. The freedom of private business to operate competitively for profit without undue government intervention is called ______________________.
20. The economic system with private ownership and competitive distribution of goods in a free market is called ______________________.

Write the letter for the *incorrect* answer on each line (each answer, 3 points).

21. Changes brought about by the Industrial Revolution included __________.
    a. increased production
    b. faster distribution
    c. improved economy
    d. higher unemployment

22. Corporations found success in using __________.
    a. modern machinery
    b. superior production methods
    c. disciplined organization
    d. fewer laborers

23. Industrial reforms came about mainly by ____________.
   a. collective bargaining
   b. democratic passing of laws
   c. forceful overthrow of capitalists
   d. peaceful negotiations

24. War affects industry by ____________.
   a. decreasing unemployment
   b. increasing production
   c. increasing the demand for military equipment
   d. lowering profits

25. Factors influencing the rise of socialism include ____________.
   a. *Das Kapital*
   b. abuse of proletariat
   c. fall of capitalism
   d. Marx's theories

Answer these questions (each answer, 5 points).

26. What three basic requirements must a nation have for industry to grow?
   a. ____
   b. ____
   c. ____

27. Give three factors that helped to answer the cries of factory workers, improving their poor working conditions.
   a. ____
   b. ____
   c. ____

92 / 115

Score ______
Teacher check ______________
Initial Date

Name ________________________

Match these items (each answer, 2 points).

1. __________ nationalism
2. __________ imperialism
3. __________ blitzkrieg
4. __________ kamikaze
5. __________ Fourteen Points
6. __________ League of Nations
7. __________ Treaty of Versailles
8. __________ Central Powers
9. __________ United Nations
10. __________ NATO
11. __________ Berlin Airlift
12. __________ Atlantic Charter

a. Roosevelt's organization for world peace settlements
b. supply of goods to isolated Berlin
c. Germany and Austria-Hungary
d. post-World War I peace organization
e. document stating Britain's and America's goals in World War II
f. World War I peace treaty for Germany
g. loyalty to one's country
h. Russian war tactic
i. German war strategy
j. Wilson's proposals for World War I peace
k. colonization for profit
l. organization for defense against communism
m. Japanese suicide mission

Complete these sentences (each answer, 3 points).

13. Prior to World War I the balance of power in Europe was upset by Bismarck's formation of the ________________________ Alliance.
14. Famous American generals of World War II were Eisenhower in a. ________________________ and b. ________________________ in the Pacific.
15. The assassination of Archduke Ferdinand led to the start of ________________________.
16. The German bombing of the *Lusitania* brought the ________________________ into World War I.
17. British Prime Minister a. ________________________ and President b. ________________________ met often to plan Allied strategy in World War II.
18. Hitler and Mussolini raised their countries' economies by building up their ________________________.
19. Hitler's invasion of Poland led to ________________________.
20. The American President who fought for world peace following World War I with his Fourteen Points and League of Nations was ________________________.
21. Fascism and Communism were both ________________________ governments that completely controlled their people.
22. American entrance into World War II was forced by the Japanese attack on ________________________.

Answer *true* or *false* (each answer, 1 point).

23. ____________ Bismarck worked to isolate France from possible allies.
24. ____________ In World War I, Germany launched a huge French offensive to win the war before Americans joined the Allies.
25. ____________ The Allied drive of 1918 forced the Germans out of Western Europe and brought them to surrender.
26. ____________ President Wilson's theories of a just peace met strong opposition in World War I peace talks.
27. ____________ America made so many loans to Europe that when the Great Depression struck, it was felt world-wide.
28. ____________ Germany, Japan, and France were the aggressive nations in pre-World War II years.
29. ____________ World War II in the Pacific was mainly naval, with land fighting carried out by the army.
30. ____________ Russia's withdrawal from World War II after the Russian Revolution strengthened the German cause.
31. ____________ World War II peace settlements were constantly deadlocked between the United States and Russia.
32. ____________ The United Nations and NATO were determined in their strong stand against Communism.

Write the letter for the correct answer on each line (each answer, 2 points).

33. The event that finally brought the German defeat in World War I was ____________.
    a. America's entrance into the war
    b. the Normandy invasion
    c. the Allied drive of 1918
    d. the stand at Chateau-Thierry

34. The terms of the Treaty of Versailles preventing Germany from again rising to power included ____________.
    a. the withdrawal of occupation troops from Germany
    b. reparations payments to Germany
    c. limitations on German army and navy
    d. the division of Berlin

35. Post-World War I conditions in Germany were characterized by ____________.
    a. prosperity
    b. bitterness
    c. pleasure-seeking
    d. economic growth

36. World War II Allied offensive strategy in the Pacific included ____________.
    a. the Sino-Japanese War
    b. the Normandy invasion
    c. island-hopping toward Japan
    d. land invasion of Japan

37. In establishing World War II peace treaties, Allied nations ____________.
    a. agreed over reparations
    b. fought totalitarianism
    c. left German industry crippled
    d. set boundaries and territory ownership

Answer these questions (each answer, 5 points).

38. What conditions led to the following wars?

a. World War I ______________________________

____

____

b. World War II ______________________________

____

____

39. What factions brought disagreement in settling the peace after these wars?

a. World War I ______________________________

____

____

b. World War II ______________________________

____

____

80 / 100

Score ______

Teacher check ______________
Initial Date

Name ____________________

Match these items. Answers can be used more than once or not at all. (each answer, 1 point)

1. ________ Joseph Stalin
2. ________ Harry Truman
3. ________ Lech Walesa
4. ________ Ho Chi Minh
5. ________ Gamal Abdel Nasser
6. ________ Juan Peron
7. ________ Fidel Castro
8. ________ Nelson Mandela
9. ________ Ronald Reagan
10. ________ Nikita Khrushchev

a. China
b. Soviet Union
c. United States
d. Poland
e. Argentina
f. Egypt
g. Cuba
h. Vietnam
i. South Africa
j. Mongolia

Name the continent in which each country is located (2 points per answer).

11. ____________________ Vietnam
12. ____________________ Latvia
13. ____________________ Egypt
14. ____________________ Ecuador
15. ____________________ Canada
16. ____________________ India
17. ____________________ Namibia
18. ____________________ Taiwan
19. ____________________ Poland
20. ____________________ Greenland

Choose a name from the list to complete the sentences. Two are not used. (1 point per answer)

Congo	Andes	Nile
Sahara	Amazon	Everest
Superior	Tigris	Alps
Atlas	Himalaya	Gobi

21. The ____________________ River covers much of the interior of central Africa.
22. The largest desert in the world is the ____________________ in northern Africa.
23. The ____________________ Mountains run along the west coast of South America.
24. The ____________________ and Euphrates Rivers were the birthplace of the Sumerian, Assyrian, and Babylonian civilizations in Asia.
25. Mount ____________________ is the tallest mountain in the world.

26. The ______________________________ River is the longest in the world.

27. The ______________________________ Mountains are in central Asia in the area of Nepal.

28. The ______________________________ are mountains in Europe.

29. The desert in the Asian country of Mongolia is the ______________________________.

30. The ______________________________ River in South America has the world's largest drainage basin.

Answer the following questions (Points per question are noted in the parentheses).

31. Describe the American strategy during the Cold War. (4 points)

____

____

____

____

32. How were the Korean and Vietnam Wars similar? (4 points)

____

____

____

____

33. What was the outcome of the Korean War? (4 points)

____

____

____

____

34. What was détente? (2 points)

____

____

____

____

35. What did the Iron Curtain separate? (2 points)

____

____

____

____

36. What was the Cold War? When did it begin and end? (4 points)

____

____

____

____

37. Describe the Cuban Missile Crisis. (4 points)

____

____

____

____

Complete the following (2 points per question).

38. North and South America are connected by ____________________.

39. Name two nations that did not exist in 1989: a. ____________________ and b. ____________________.

40. The Chinese communist leader who started the Cultural Revolution was ____________________.

41. The Security Council at the ____________________ is responsible for world peace, but only in the General Assembly are all of the nations represented.

42. The most infamous symbol of the Cold War in Europe, the ____________________ ,in Germany was torn down in 1989.

43. The Warsaw Pact was formed by the Soviet Union to counter the Cold War alliance of the Western countries which was called ____________________.

44. The ____________________ gave millions of dollars to European countries to help them rebuild after World War II and prevent communist expansion.

45. Name two countries that were still communist as of the mid-1990s: a. ____________________ and b. ____________________

46. Name the largest and smallest continents: a. ____________________ and b. ____________________.

47. The agreement between Canada, the United States, and Mexico to eliminate tariffs and create a free trade zone is called ____________________.

Choose the letter that best describes the term given. (1 point per answer).

48. __________ SALT
49. __________ European Union
50. __________ Solidarity
51. __________ Sputnik
52. __________ perestroika
53. __________ satellites
54. __________ Berlin airlift
55. __________ Pusan Perimeter
56. __________ U-2 Incident
57. __________ Prague Spring

a. Soviet reform begun in the 1980s
b. line held by South Koreans after the North's first attack in the Korean War
c. name for the European communist nations
d. a type of United States of Europe
e. reform in Czechoslovakia in the 1960s
f. American response to the Berlin Blockade
g. the first satellite to orbit the earth
h. treaty to limit nuclear weapons
i. the shooting down of an American spy plane over the Soviet Union
j. independent Polish trade union of the 1980s

Answer *true* or *false* (1 point per answer).

58. ______________ South American countries were all prosperous democracies during the Cold War.
59. ______________ Communism ended in most of Europe in 1989.
60. ______________ The peace talks to end the Korean War stalled over the issue of territory.
61. ______________ The Soviet Union was very passive and non-threatening during the Cold War.
62. ______________ Vietnam was reunited by force under a communist government in the 1970s.
63. ______________ The United States often supported dictators during the Cold War because they were anti-communist.

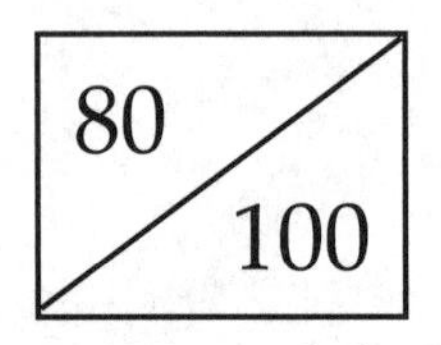

Score ______
Teacher check ______________
Initial Date

Name ______________________________

Match these items (each answer, 2 points).

1. __________ Hebrews
2. __________ Egyptians
3. __________ Babylonians
4. __________ Chinese
5. __________ Greeks
6. __________ Romans
7. __________ Italy
8. __________ England
9. __________ France
10. __________ Spain

a. ruled by family of bankers, the Medicis
b. agricultural civilization; used clay for building, beautiful capital city
c. parliamentary government
d. oldest early civilization
e. rulers threatened by Huguenot opposition
f. earliest civilization in the Far East
g. nation whose power in the New World declined as precious metals were depleted
h. first democratic and representative government
i. became a Republic when dissatisfaction with the king arose among the plebeians
j. the location of huge lakes of oil
k. people through whom God gave the Old Testament to the world

Write the letter for the correct answer on each line (each answer, 2 points).

11. Napoleon was defeated at the battle of ____________.
    a. Trenton
    b. Waterloo
    c. Bull Run
    d. Gettysburg

12. The cotton gin was the invention of ____________.
    a. Eli Whitney
    b. Johann Gutenberg
    c. James Watt
    d. George Stephenson

13. World War I was precipitated by the ____________.
    a. intervention of England into European affairs
    b. bombing of Pearl Harbor
    c. Triple Alliance
    d. assassination of Archduke Francis Ferdinand

14. The main body of the United Nations is the ____________.
    a. General Assembly
    b. Security Council
    c. Secretariat
    d. International Court of Justice

15. A military alliance between Western nations is the ____________.
    a. United Nations
    b. North Atlantic Treaty Organization
    c. Commonwealth of Nations
    d. European Communities

16. The war involving Rome and Phoenicia over the city of Carthage was the ____________.
    a. Peloponnesian War
    b. French and Indian War
    c. Punic War
    d. Battle of Hastings

17. Missions to recapture the Holy Land were known as the ____________.
    a Crusades
    b. Reformation
    c. Ides of March
    d. Dark Ages

18. A statement passed in 1628 by the English Parliament that no one could be taxed without Parliament's consent was the ____________.
    a. Magna Carta
    b. Petition of Right
    c. Peace of Westphalia
    d. Gunpowder Act

19. Mass production in factories to provide cheaper goods was perfected by ____________.
    a. Cyrus McCormick
    b. George Stephenson
    c. Jethro Wood
    d. Henry Ford

20. The United States entered World War I when ____________.
    a. Archduke Ferdinand was shot
    b. Pearl Harbor was bombed
    c. the Germans attacked the Lusitania
    d. the Germans marched across Belgium

Match these items (each answer, 2 points).

21. __________ Pericles
22. __________ Caesar
23. __________ Augustus
24. __________ Charlemagne
25. __________ King Ferdinand and Queen Isabella
26. __________ Petrarch
27. __________ Machiavelli
28. __________ Leonardo da Vinci
29. __________ Copernicus
30. __________ John Wycliffe

a. reign began with Roman peace
b. rulers of Spain
c. Athens reached its peak
d. left to rule alone after the Roman triumverate dissolved
e. *The Prince*
f. father of humanism in Italy
g. leader of the Franks
h. proved the sun was the center of the solar system
i. invented gunpowder
j. wrote of clerical abuses
k. painted the *Mona Lisa*

Answer *true* or *false* (each answer, 1 point).

31. ____________ During medieval times the Catholic Church dictated to the people in almost every matter.

32. ____________ In defiance of the absolute power of the king, people's representatives in England declared themselves a National Assembly.

33. ____________ Napoleon's government was a dictatorship.

34. ____________ The Clayton Antitrust Act curbed the trend toward business monopolies in the United States.

35. ____________ World War II began as a result of Hitler's attack on France.

36. ____________ The Middle East has declined as a dominant force since World War II.

37. ______________ John Knox was a Scottish Presbyterian who converted to Catholicism during the Reformation.

38. ______________ The two most powerful Tudor monarchs were Henry VIII and Elizabeth I.

39. ______________ During World War II, the Americans fought alone in the Pacific.

40. ______________ The economic importance of the Middle East today is agriculture.

Complete these activities (each answer, 3 points).

41. The Egyptians are credited with the development of a. ______________________________,
b. ______________________________, c. ______________________________, and
d. ______________________________.

42. The divine right of kings to rule a country is ______________________________.

43. Three groups of religious thought in France were a. ______________________________,
b. ______________________________, and c. ______________________________.

44. A system of government intervention to increase national trade and prosperity is
______________________________.

45. The first American Constitution was called the ______________________________.

80 / 100

Score ______
Teacher check ______________
Initial Date

LIFEPAC

ANSWER KEYS

SECTION ONE

1.1 cities
1.2 large population of nonfarmers; enough food
1.3 Any order:
  a. technology
  b. division of labor
  c. political organization
  d. higher moral codes
  or arts and literature, commerce and trade, bookkeeping and accounting
1.4 the tools and processes to make things and to satisfy human needs
1.5 It made food production more efficient.
1.6 labor
1.7 primitive
1.8 state
1.9 evolution
1.10 progressive
1.11 perversion
1.12 true
1.13 true
1.14 false
1.15 true
1.16 true
1.17 true
1.18 false
1.19 true
1.20 true
1.21 c
1.22 e
1.23 a
1.24 b
1.25 f
1.26 innocence
1.27 language
1.28 c
1.29 a
1.30 b
1.31 a
1.32 d
1.33 a
1.34 Cain became a farmer, Abel a shepherd.
1.35 trade
1.36 Cain's
1.37 Any order:
  a. tent dwellers
  b. musicians
  c. workmen in brass and iron
1.38 because of the Flood's destructiveness
1.39 in its heathen theology and idolatry
1.40 the *Gilgamesh Epic*
1.41 special revelation; the huge boat
1.42 teacher check
1.43 a. that it was because of intermarriage between Cainites and Sethites
  b. that it was because of intermarriage between fallen angels and humans
1.44 teacher check
1.45 Salvation: ark = Christ; Flood = judgment; those in the ark = those in Christ
1.46 yes or no
1.47 because everyone is descended from them
1.48 true
1.49 true
1.50 true
1.51 false
1.52 false
1.53 true
1.54 d
1.55 b
1.56 a
1.57 d
1.58 b
1.59 e
1.60 f
1.61 a
1.62 c
1.63 d
1.64 united human strength in rebellion against God
1.65 Indo-European
1.66 Any order:
  a. Akkadian
  b. Aramaic
  c. Syriac
  d. Phoenician
  e. Ugaritic
  f. Hebrew
  g. Moabite
  or Arabic, Minean, Sabaean, Ethiopic
1.67 no
1.68 to serve Shem and Japheth
1.69 with a civilization built upon the Bible and Christ
1.70 Medes
1.71 Africa
1.72 Semites
1.73 genetic
1.74 11
1.75 Greeks
1.76 Canaanite
1.77 Ham or Mizraim

1.78 from the Persian Gulf to the Mediterranean Sea
1.79 Third Dynasty of Ur
1.80 a planned economy
1.81 around 2161 B.C.
1.82 northwest of Ur along the Euphrates
1.83 a secular ruler; King
1.84 idolators
1.85 Any order:
a. descendants
b. blessing
c. nation
d. land
1.86 Jesus Christ

SECTION TWO

2.1 along the Nile and its delta
2.2 desert
2.3 Any order:
a. Red Sea
b. Mediterranean Sea
c. Libya
d. Nubia
2.4 because the Nile gave it all its water
2.5 Lower Egypt is from the delta to past Memphis. Upper Egypt is the rest of the area.
2.6-2.8 B.C.

3500 3000 2500 2000 1500 1000

Old Kingdom (3000–2200) Middle Kingdom (2200–1650) New Kingdom (1650–1050)

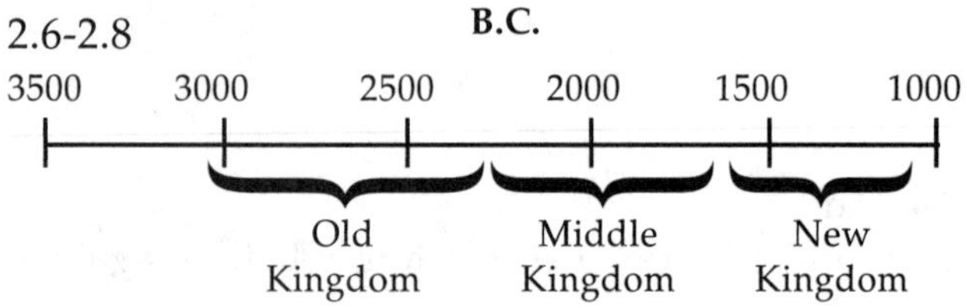

2.9 l
2.10 d
2.11 k
2.12 f
2.13 j
2.14 a
2.15 g
2.16 c
2.17 h
2.18 i
2.19 b
2.20 b
2.21 c
2.22 a
2.23 c
2.24 a
2.25 They were Semitic Asians, probably beginning in Lower Egypt and moving to Ithet-Tawy.
2.26 one of the Hyksos
2.27 140 years
2.28 The New Kingdom
2.29 Ahmose I of Thebes
2.30 1250 B.C.
2.31 1250 B.C.
2.32 Akhenaten
2.33 Aten
2.34 yes
2.35 the state god of Egypt
2.36 the army
2.37 Ramses I
2.38 Syria
2.39 Hatshepsut
2.40 woman
2.41 self
2.42 Moses
2.43 Hatshepsut
2.44 true
2.45 true
2.46 false
2.47 true
2.48 false
2.49 false
2.50 true
2.51 true
2.52 a
2.53 b
2.54 a
2.55 d
2.56 a
2.57 b
2.58 b
2.59 Any order:
a. prime minister
b. chief justice
c. treasurer
2.60 Any order:
a. aristocracy
b. middle classes
c. lower classes
2.61 Hamito-Semitic

2.62 3100
2.63 Any order:
a. hieroglyphic
b. hieratic
c. demotic
2.64 Rosetta
2.65 They were the first to have literature for its own sake rather than for its religious or utilitarian value.
2.66 *Pyramid Texts*
2.67 yes
2.68 Any order:
a. sculpture
b. bas-relief
c. painting
d. jewelry making
2.69 belief in or worship of more than one god
2.70 Any order:
a. Re—the sun god
b. Osiris—the god of the Nile and fertility
c. Isis—the goddess of nature
2.71 Either order:
a. The "divine" pharaoh controlled them psychologically.
b. They were highly moral.

SECTION THREE

3.1 d
3.2 c
3.3 a
3.4 as an upholder of the common people
3.5 his law code
3.6 governmentally controlled
3.7 Hammurabi's laws were man-centered while Moses' laws were God-centered.
3.8 Any order:
a. multiplication
b. division
c. square and cube roots
d. algebraic equation
e. geometry
f. concept of zero (0) or place value
3.9 Either order:
a. zero
b. place value
3.10 *Gilgamesh Epic*
3.11 Asia Minor in 1800 B.C.
3.12 law codes and iron smelting
3.13 north of Babylonia on the Mesopotamian plain along the Tigris
3.14 from the Persian Gulf to the Mediterranean Sea and from the Caucasus to the Nile
3.15 c
3.16 a
3.17 a
3.18 c
3.19 a
3.20 c
3.21 d
3.22 c
3.23 a
3.24 b
3.25 c
3.26 b
3.27 d
3.28 c
3.29 b
3.30 Ashur
3.31 his regent on earth
3.32 Ishtar
3.33 the god of wisdom
3.34 cuneiform
3.35 clay
3.36 library
3.37 Any order:
a. wall paintings
b. bas-reliefs
c. statues
d. cylinder seals
e. ivory carvings
f. metal work
3.38 kings of Assyria
3.39 c
3.40 e
3.41 b
3.42 a
3.43 d
3.44 Nabopolassar
3.45 Egypt
3.46 Daniel

3.47 Jeremiah

3.48 3

3.49 Jehoiachin

3.50 Jehoiachin

3.51 God

3.52 Jerusalem

3.53 70

3.54 Belshazzar

3.55 539

3.56 Any order:
a. Anu
b. Eulil
c. Ea

3.57 Ishtar

3.58 the sun in his strength, the god of power justice, and war

3.59 the Amorites

3.60 the *Babylonian Chronicles*

SECTION FOUR

4.1 c

4.2 d

4.3 a

4.4 c

4.5 d

4.6 a

4.7 c

4.8 b

4.9 b

4.10 Any order:
a. Ezra
b. Zerubbabel
c. Nehemiah
d. Joshua
e. Shashbazzer

4.11 Any order:
a. Zechariah
b. Haggai
c. Malachi

4.12 Either order:
a. Ezra
b. Nehemiah

4.13 gods of nature, fertility, and the heavens

4.14 He believed in doing good, not evil.
He worshiped one god, Ahara-mazda.

4.15 Roman

4.16 Any order:
a. Susa
b. Ecbatana
c. Babylon
d. Persepolis

4.17 satraps

4.18 post

SECTION ONE

1.1 a. Kithar and Sulaiman ranges
b. Himalayas
c. Arabian Sea
d. Bay of Bengel, Burma
e. Indian Ocean

1.2 Any order:
a. Ganges
b. Krishna
c. Narbada

1.3 b

1.4 a

1.5 b

1.6 d

1.7 d

1.8 a

1.9 c

1.10 those who were outside the caste system

1.11 Alexander the Great

1.12 the Mauryan dynasty

1.13 Nomadic tribes invaded India from central Asia.

1.14 Sanskrit

1.15 *Vedas*

1.16 wisdom

1.17 *Upanishads*

1.18 Homer

1.19 true

1.20 false

1.21 true

1.22 true

1.23 true

1.24 false

1.25 true

1.26 Either order:
a. Yangtze
b. Hwang Ho

1.27 1500 B.C.

1.28 Chou

1.29 Wu Ti

1.30 a 200-year period of peace

1.31 he built the Great Wall of China

1.32 bronze

1.33 Chou

1.34 confucius

1.35 li

1.36 rebel

1.37 social

1.38 father

1.39 nature

1.40 Han

SECTION TWO

2.1 d

2.2 a

2.3 b

2.4 c

2.5 b

2.6 a

2.7 d

2.8 c

2.9 a

2.10 c

2.11 b

2.12 invasions or migrations

2.13 Either order:
a. Athens
b. Sparta

2.14 Either order:
a. poor soil for farming
b. overpopulation of city-states

2.15 Great Greece

2.16 Helots

2.17 state

2.18 Any order:
  a. self-control
  b. modesty
  c. strict obedience

2.19 Either order:
  a. Nazi Germany
  b. communist Russia

2.20 Any order:
  a. Spain
  b. Italy
  c. Sicily or Egypt

2.21 Byzantium

2.22 memorization

2.23 God

2.24 Athens

2.25 Greek poet

2.26 an archon

2.27 dictatorial

2.28 Lydia or Lydians

2.29 There were slaves. Lower classes could not vote. Women had limited rights.

2.30 to record names for possible banishment

2.31 a person who came to power outside constitutional means

2.32 He advanced the cause of democracy more than any other Greek ruler by changing the basis of representation in government from family groups to territories.

2.33 He made the first world map.

2.34 g

2.35 d

2.36 b

2.37 a

2.38 e

2.39 c

2.40 h

2.41 Pericles

2.42 Cleisthenes

2.43 commerce

2.44 temple

2.45 Either order:
  a. Aeschylus
  b. Aristophanes

2.46 histories

2.47 arrogance

2.48 Corinth

2.49 b

2.50 a

2.51 d

2.52 b

2.53 b

2.54 c

2.55 a

2.56 b

2.57 a

2.58 d

2.59 false

2.60 true

2.61 true

2.62 false

2.63 false

2.64 true

2.65 true

2.66 false

2.67 false

2.68 Any order:
  a. thinker
  b. soldier
  c. athlete
  d. attractive

2.69 Egypt. It was destined to be the intellectual center of the Mediterranean world.

2.70 to fuse East and West into one empire

2.71 bad habits of drinking and eating

2.72 It was divided into three parts.

2.73 323 B.C. to 31 B.C.

2.74 Greek

2.75 Rome

2.76 b

2.77 d

2.78 c

2.79 c

2.80 d

2.81 c

2.82 c

2.83 d

2.84 b

2.85 c

2.86 b

2.87 d
2.88 b
2.89 c
2.90 a
2.91 c
2.92 d
2.93 a
2.94 false
2.95 true
2.96 false
2.97 true
2.98 false
2.99 false
2.100 true

SECTION THREE

3.1 Any order:
a. Pre-Republic
b. Republic
c. Empire
3.2 Either order:
a. Romulus
b. Remus
3.3 Etruscans
3.4 family
3.5 one woman
3.6 b
3.7 d
3.8 a
3.9 d
3.10 c
3.11 b
3.12 b
3.13 d
3.14 b
3.15 c
3.16 a
3.17 d
3.18 a
3.19 c
3.20 b
3.21 Greece
3.22 Colosseum
3.23 Forum
3.24 aqueducts
3.25 Virgil
3.26 intellectual
3.27 e
3.28 f
3.29 b
3.30 a
3.31 d
3.32 Mark Antony
3.33 14
3.34 Nero
3.35 Either order:
a. China
b. India
3.36 305
3.37 peace
3.38 Augustus
3.39 Roman Law
3.40 Latin
3.41 leadership dispute
decline in trade hurt the economy
mercenaries hired
3.42 true
3.43 false
3.44 false
3.45 true
3.46 false
3.47 true
3.48 false
3.49 true
3.50 true
3.51 false
3.52 false
3.53 true
3.54 true
3.55 true
3.56 true
3.57 Either order:
a. trade routes
b. highway systems
3.58 tolerance
3.59 Emperor Decius
3.60 Trinity
3.61 constantine, Nicene
3.62 metropolitan
3.63 false
3.64 false
3.65 false
3.66 true
3.67 false
3.68 a.
3.69 c.
3.70 d.
3.71 e.
3.72 b.

SECTION ONE

1.1 Any order:
 a. Ostrogoths
 b. Franks
 c. Anglo-Saxons

1.2 Attila the Hun

1.3 Any order:
 a. compensation
 b. trial by ordeal (or combat)
 c. oath swearing

1.4 Arian

1.5 d

1.6 i

1.7 h

1.8 g

1.9 b

1.10 c

1.11 e

1.12 k

1.13 f

1.14 a

1.15 Example: Ostrogothic more Roman, Frankish almost purely Germanic, Anglo-Saxon combination of several cultures- Roman, Celtic, native Briton, and Anglo-Saxon

1.16 Justinian

1.17 Byzantine

1.18 Belisarius

1.19 b

1.20 c

1.21 a

1.22 e

1.23 a

1.24 f

1.25 b

1.26 d

SECTION TWO

2.1 Do-Nothing-Kings

2.2 a. Christmas Day
 b. 800
 c. Leo III

2.3 travel in pairs through the empire checking on courts and the state of the empire

2.4 counties

2.5 frontier or border areas

2.6 c

2.7 a

2.8 b

2.9 c

2.10 b

2.11 d

2.12 Beowulf

2.13 Venerable Bede

2.14 c

2.15 Justinian

2.16 a. Constantinople
 b. culture

2.17 b

2.18 c

2.19 e

2.20 a

2.21 d

2.22 c

SECTION THREE

3.1 j

3.2 c

3.3 g

3.4 b

3.5 k

3.6 a

3.7 i

3.8 f

3.9 h

3.10 d

3.11 a system of local government where a vassal would give an allegiance to a lord in exchange for the use of some land

3.12 a social and economic system where serfs were bound to a manor ruled by a lord

3.13 a standard of conduct for the ideal knight

3.14 c

3.15 a

3.16 b

3.17 c

3.18 b

3.19 b

3.20 d

3.21 a

3.22 f

3.23 c

3.24 dispute of the succession to the throne of France; throne claimed by both Philip VI of France and Edward III of England

3.25 dispute between the houses of York and Lancaster over English throne

3.26 Hint: Answers should include feudal system had made some monasteries rich; monks vowed to poverty, did not like this; began new monasteries with stricter rules; accepted no fiefs.

3.27 Franciscans and Dominicans Orders of Friars, or brothers, who worked as missionaries, fought heresies and earned or begged for their livelihood

3.28 a. Philip Augustus
b. King John

3.29 Francis of Assisi

3.30 *Summa Theologica*

3.31 a. Fourth Crusade or Crusaders
b. 1204

3.32 Any order:
a. internal power struggles
b. invasions
c. loss of trade **or** capture of Constantinople **or** Black Plague

3.33 a. Constantinople
b. Turks
c. 1453

3.34 Constantine XI

3.35 e

3.36 h

3.37 a

3.38 j

3.39 b

3.40 f

3.41 d

3.42 k

3.43 c

3.44 g

SECTION ONE

1.1 a period of transition or change bridging the gap between medieval and modern times

1.2 Any order:
a. growth of trade and wealth
b. rise of the middle class
c. the decline of feudalism
d. the return to early Greek and Roman ideas

1.3 Any order:
a. government
b. literature and thought
c. the arts
d. science

1.4 c

1.5 b

1.6 d

1.7 a

1.8 a

1.9 national government (or country or France)

1.10 Charles VII

1.11 burned at the stake as a witch and heretic

1.12 national power

1.13 Louis XI

1.14 true

1.15 true

1.16 false

1.17 true

1.18 false

1.19 false

1.20 false

1.21 true

1.22 a duke or ruler

1.23 a government ruled by only a privileged few

1.24 a Florentine Dominican friar who attacked church corruption and was excommunicated and executed as a heretic

1.25 ruling assembly of 200 merchants and bankers in Venice. It was a very efficient form of government.

1.26 ruler of the Duchy of Milan

1.27 the most powerful political family in Italy; they were wealthy and sponsored many famous artists

1.28 a gold coin used as the standard for Europe

1.29 b

1.30 f

1.31 e

1.32 a

1.33 c

1.34 the Reconquista

1.35 Any order:
a. Castile and Leon
b. Portugal
c. Aragon

1.36 the Almohades

1.37 a. Ferdinand
b. Isabella

1.38 Any 4, any order:
a. a greater national unity
b. the establishment of the Inquisition
c. a royal police force which restored civil peace
d. the recapture of Grenada or the conversion or expulsion of the Jews and Moors, the spread of Spanish influence through trade and expansion

1.39 a. faith
b. territory

1.40 Any order:
a. Gothic
b. Romanesque
c. Byzantine

1.41 Gothic

1.42 Romanesque

1.43 Saint Basil's in Moscow or Hagia Sophia in Constantinople

1.44 Either order:
a. Inigo Jones
b. Michelangelo

1.45 e

1.46 a

1.47 f

1.48 b

1.49 c

1.50 f

1.51 f

1.52 d

1.53 g

1.54 h

1.55 c

1.56 Any one:
realistic
natural
lifelike

1.57 religious

1.58 da Vinci

1.59 oil paint

1.60 Dürer

1.61 c

1.62 b

1.63 a

1.64 a

1.65 b

1.66 Either order:
a. Sir Thomas More
b. Francis Bacon

1.67 Any order:
a. Sidney
b. Spenser
c. Drayton

1.68 b-d any order:
a. Shakespeare
b. comedies
c. histories
d. tragedies

1.69 Ben Jonson

1.70 cloak and sword (dagger)

1.71 *Don Quixote (Don Quixote de la Mancha)*

1.72 a. wrote a book (*Opus Majus*), encouraged experimentation, described eyeglasses
b. contributed to the fields of botany, anatomy, engineering and geology. He sketched muscle and bone. He drew inventions for man's flight and various weapons and machines. He studied rock and water (geology) and developed canals and locks.
c. heliocentric theory. He wrote a book about heliocentrism.
d. discovered concept of specific gravity laws of pendulum. In astronomy he invented telescopes and discovered four satellites around Jupiter. He found that the moon was rough and only reflected light.
e. discovered that planetary orbits were oval, not circular. He also discovered three laws of planetary motion.
f. discovered laws of gravity and motion; discovered aspects of light and color, leading to today's spectrum analysis

1.73 teacher check

SECTION TWO

2.1 granting favors or appointments to one's own relatives

2.2 obtaining a church office by paying for it

2.3 a papal bull or official statement of the pope declaring the pope as head of both church and state

2.4 Any 4, any order:
a. nepotism
b. simony
c. the Unam sanctum
d. the sale of indulgences; some of the members of the clergy neglected their church obligations while living lives of luxury.

2.5 The church held much land. The monarchs thought that they should control church holdings.

2.6 a. clerical abuses
b. papal authority

2.7 John of Gaunt

2.8 the Bible

2.9 Lollards

2.10 his translation of the Bible into English

2.11 John Huss

2.12 a. excommunicated
b. burned at the stake

2.13 unity of Brethren
or Moravian church

2.14 b

2.15 d

2.16 b

2.17 b

2.18 a

2.19 He believed in comprehensive reform of religious practices and beliefs.

He believed that the Lord's Supper symbolized Christ.

He believed in a simplified church organization, without Saints, fasting, and celibate priests.

2.20 Zurich, Switzerland

2.21 Luther tried to negotiate, Zwingli became involved in a war with them, and Zwingli died in battle.

2.22 Any order:
a. in adult baptism
b. separation of church and state
c. peace
d. no swearing

2.23 Conrad Grebel

2.24 true

2.25 false

2.26 true

2.27 false

2.28 true

2.29 true

2.30 true

2.31 false

2.32 true

2.33 Either order:
a. religious
b. political

2.34 Catherine of Aragon

2.35 a dynasty

2.36 Act of Supremacy

2.37 a rebellion

2.38 a-b either order:
a. Greek
b. Hebrew
c. English

2.39 the doctrine of the Anglican church

2.40 the church of England (Anglican)

2.41 e

2.42 h

2.43 a

2.44 g

2.45 c

2.46 f

2.47 b, d

2.48 9

2.49 council of regents

2.50 the duke of Somerset

2.51 Any order:
a. lowering the values of gold and silver because of new discoveries
b. Henry's debasement of the coin, using more alloy
c. enclosure caused the price of land to rise

2.52 Mary Tudor

2.53 Lady Jane Gray

2.54 true

2.55 true

2.56 true

2.57 false

2.58 false

2.59 false

2.60 There was a threat of civil war. Foreign relations were troubled: England resented the French influence in Scotland and was also involved with the Spanish.

2.61 She was capable and shrewd. She could deal with people and handle problems. Her survival of many plots against her had given her self-confidence. She was complex, intelligent, and willful.

2.62 true

2.63 false

2.64 false

2.65 true

2.66 a

2.67 c

2.68 b

2.69 d

2.70 teacher check

2.71 Queen Isabella's confessor

2.72 a. cardinal
b. chancellor of state
c. regent

2.73 printing of the whole Bible in the original languages—Hebrew and Greek

2.74 Ignatius Loyola

2.75 Any order:
a. poverty
b. chastity
c. obedience

2.76 military

2.77 Any 4, any order:
a. physically fit
b. intelligent
c. educated
d. of the upper class or of strong character

2.78 Any four, any order:
a. It provided for discipline and removal of clergy who abused the church.
b. It recognized the pope as the authority on doctrine.
c. It reaffirmed the seven sacraments, indulgences, purgatory, and the saints.

2.79 Any order:
a. concordats
b. the Index
c. the Inquisition

2.80 false

2.81 true

2.82 true

2.83 true

2.84 false

2.85 false

2.86 b

2.87 a

2.88 c

2.89 b

2.90 d

2.91 Any order:
a. Huguenots
b. Catholics
c. Politiques

2.92 French Calvinists

2.93 French Catholics primarily interested in politics

2.94 fleet of Spanish warships defeated by the British in 1588

2.95 German war of about 30 years over religious and political problems

2.96 restored Catholic lands and restricted Protestants, except Lutherans

2.97 Swedish leader and a Lutheran. He led a movement to oust the Hapsburgs from Germany.

2.98 brought an end to religious war in Germany. It insured rights to Calvinists and Lutherans equally, and allowed each prince as head of state to determine its own religion.

SECTION ONE

1.1 Any order:
- a. resented English intervention and aid to the Netherlands
- b. wanted to return England to the Catholic Church
- c. wanted to stop English interference with Spain's New World trade

1.2 England remained independent and Protestant. England became a sea power.

1.3 g

1.4 d

1.5 e

1.6 b

1.7 c

1.8 f

1.9 c

1.10 a

1.11 d

1.12 b

1.13 a

1.14 Any order:
- a. no taxation without parliamentary consent
- b. no one could be imprisoned without trial
- c. no soldiers would be quartered in homes during peacetime

1.15 when Charles I sent naval expeditions to aid the French Huguenots of La Rochelle

1.16 because Charles believed in the divine rights of kings and disliked the Puritans; thus Parliament was suspicious of him

1.17 Parliament

1.18
- a. knighthood
- b. monopolies
- c. fines

1.19
- a. Scotland
- b. England

1.20 Long Parliament

1.21 By custom, coastal towns gave ships to navy in emergency. Charles I asked for money.

1.22 Abolished ship money and taxes without their consent, abolished prerogative courts, and passed the Triennial Act.

1.23 Any order:
- a. political—supremacy of king or Parliament
- b. economic—new economic groups wanted role in government
- c. religious—national church or freedom for several Protestant groups

1.24 northern and western England, Catholics, moderate Anglicans, aristocracy, and conservative agricultural interest

1.25 southern and eastern England, Puritans, Presbyterians, middle class, and merchants

1.26 England's first and only constitution

1.27 It never had support of majority of England.

1.28 true

1.29 true

1.30 false

1.31 true

1.32 false

1.33 true

1.34 false

1.35 Either order:
- a. Habeas Corpus Act
- b. Whig Party and Tory Party

1.36 Either order:
- a. Test Act required officeholders to be practicing Anglicans
- b. Disabling Act barred Catholics from Parliament

1.37 Test Act

1.38 d

1.39 e

1.40 f

1.41 a

1.42 c

1.43 g

1.44 eight

1.45 Marie dè Medici

1.46 Estates General

1.47 Any order:
a. nobility
b. clergy
c. Third Estate

1.48 Richelieu

1.49 Either order:
a. to make the king all powerful in France
b. to make France supreme in Europe

1.50 intendants

1.51 Hapsburgs

1.52 Any order:
a. Spain
b. Spanish Netherlands
c. Alsace
d. Austria
e. Franche-Cometè

1.53 Thirty Years' War

1.54 bad harvests, decline in grain prices, discontent of provincial governors and officeholders encouraged by English Civil Wars.

1.55 false

1.56 true

1.57 true

1.58 false

1.59 true

1.60 true

1.61 b

1.62 a

1.63 a

1.64 c

1.65 d

1.66 teacher check

1.67 a. War: War of Devolution or War of the Spanish Netherlands
Date: 1667 to 1668
Countries involved: Spanish Netherlands, England, Sweden
Lands Acquired by France: twelve areas from Spain including Lille

b. War: The Dutch War
Date: 1672 to 1678
Countries Involved: Spanish Netherlands, Austria, Spain
Lands Acquired by France: Franche-Cometé

c. War: War of the League of Augsburg
Date: 1689 to 1697
Countries Involved: Holy Roman Empire, Spain, Sweden, German States, and England
Lands Acquired by France: Stasbourg

d. War: War of the Spanish Succession
Date: 1701 to 1713
Countries Involved: England, Dutch Netherlands, Austria, and Prussia
Lands Acquired by France: France lost Newfoundland, Nova Scotia, Hudson Bay to England. Spain ceded Gibraltar to England. Austria received Naples, Milan, and Sardinia. The Spanish Netherlands became the Austrian Netherlands

1.68 government more arbitrary—king and ministers supported by bureaucracy and army; France bankrupt and weak from wars

1.69 a system of government intervention to promote national prosperity and to increase the power of the country.

1.70 Any order:
a. the more gold and silver a country had, the more prosperous it was
b. self-sufficiency
c. colonies

1.71 export more goods than imported

1.72 Any order:
a. high tariffs to reduce imports
b. bounties on exports
c. encourage manufacturing to produce as many goods as possible

1.73 The first required colonial exports to be carried in English ships. The second required exports go to England first before continental ports.

1.74 Part ownership was acquired by buying shares which were the wealth of the company. Profits depended on success and share of stocks. If the company failed, one was responsible only for his share.

1.75 Italian

1.76 Russia

1.77 a. Italian
b. England

1.78 Nova Scotia, Canada

1.79 Either order:
a. Martin Frobisher
b. John Davis

1.80 Sir Francis Drake

1.81 Either order:
a. Hudson Bay
b. The Hudson River

1.82 Any order:
a. Plymouth
b. Massachusetts Bay
c. Connecticut
d. Rhode Island
e. Maryland
f. Pennsylvania
g. Delaware
h. Carolinas

1.83 Either order:
a. New York
b. New Jersey

1.84 Jamestown

1.85 English East Indian Company

1.86 Foreign trade was encouraged and the manufacture of textiles. Subsidies and monopolies are also established.

1.87 Quebec

1.88 fur

1.89 Louis XIV

1.90 a. Caribbean
b. sugar plantations

1.91 Either order:
a. business practices
b. product quality

1.92 Most people did not want to emigrate, government did not encourage it, non-Catholics were excluded, and land system discouraged small farmers.

1.93 to compete with the English East India Company.

1.94 c

1.95 c

1.96 control of the Ohio valley

1.97 The expanded trade enriched English merchants, and the raw materials would give England an advantage in the Industrial Revolution.

SECTION TWO

2.1 Any order:
a. explore
b. obtain wealth
c. spread the Gospel

2.2 a. East Indies
b. Africa

2.3 a. Bartholomew Dias
b. Cape of Storms

2.4 a. Cape of Good Hope
b. proved to be a route to the East

2.5 circumnavigating

2.6 a

2.7 a

2.8 c

2.9 c

2.10 a

2.11 Any order:
a. lack of resources
b. lack of population
c. lack of size
d. conquest by Spain in 1580

2.12 Example:
Portugal was mainly interested in trade with Brazil and with forts and trade stations throughout the world.

2.13 Hint:
Answer should include Asian countries such as China, Japan, Sumatra, and Java, as well as Africa and the New World.

2.14 teacher check

2.15 true

2.16 false

2.17 true

2.18 true

2.19 false

2.20 true

2.21 true

2.22 teacher check

2.23 d

2.24 f

2.25 c

2.26 j

2.27 a

2.28 h

2.29 g

2.30 i

2.31 b

2.32 Hint:
Answer should include a description of the religion, the cities, and agricultural and trade practices.

2.33 Hint:
Answer should include an idea of the power and control of the Incan government.

2.34 teacher check

2.35 Either order:
a. king
b. Council of the Indies

2.36 a. Peru
b. New Spain
c. New Granada
d. la Plata
e. Lima
f. Mexico City
g. Bogotá
h. Buenos Aires

2.37 a. *encomienda*
b. peonage

2.38 Catholic Church

2.39 Any order:
a. peninsulares
b. creoles (aristocracy)
c. mestizos, mulattoes, Indians, and blacks

2.40 true

2.41 true

2.42 true

2.43 false

2.44 false

2.45 true

2.46 Example:
The Council was the governing body. It made the laws and decrees, and appointed civil workers. In times of a weak king, the Council had absolute control.

2.47 Example:
The Creoles were the aristocracy, or landowning nobles. They made their living by farming. They were the most dissatisfied with the system of government.

2.48 Example:
The church was responsible for missionizing the Indians. It opened schools for them and protected them from the *encomiendas*. It was rewarded with land and *encomiendas*.

2.49 Hint:
Answer should include the fact that he was the last of the Spanish Hapsburgs, the war of the Spanish Succession, and a reference to the balance of power. It should also mention territory lost by Spain.

2.50 Hint:
Answer should include the fact that Spain lost large sums of money and that the Counter-Reformation suffered a serious blow.

SECTION THREE

3.1 a. Protestantism
b. Islam

3.2 a. Pragmatic Sanction
b. Maria Theresa

3.3 Either order; a and b:
a. France
b. Spain
c. England

3.4 Silesia

3.5 Treaty of Aix-la-Chapelle

3.6 Any order:
a. Russia
b. Prussia
c. Austria

3.7 Balkans

3.8 teacher check

3.9 parent check

3.10 a. Spain
b. Austria

3.11 Either order:
a. French
b. Hapsburgs

3.12 Either order:
a. wealthy
b. independent

3.13 Any order:
a. the papacy
b. Venice
c. the Piedman-Savoy

3.14 baroque

3.15 a. stringed
b. opera

3.16 Either order:
a. Galileo
b. Capernicus

3.17 true

3.18 true

3.19 false

3.20 false

3.21 false

3.22 false

3.23 true

3.24 false

3.25 Hint:
Answer should include the rise of European competition, New World intrusion into commercial agriculture, the inability of the Turks to change to a manufacturing system, and internal corruption.

3.26 Answer should include information about the Shi'a sect, the military advances of Safavi, and a description of the Safavi Empire.

3.27 a

3.28 c

3.29 g

3.30 b

3.31 i

3.32 e

3.33 h

3.34 d

SECTION ONE

1.1 Tudor

1.2 Stuart

1.3 Shakespeare

1.4 human problems

1.5 Spanish Armada

1.6 divine right

1.7 King James Version

1.8 Long Parliament

1.9 a. Cavaliers
b. Roundheads

1.10 true

1.11 false

1.12 true

1.13 false

1.14 true

1.15 strong followers of the French theologian, John Calvin, who wanted to purify the Church of England from its Catholic rituals

1.16 Calvinists who wished to remain in the Anglican Church, purifying it from the inside

1.17 Calvinists wanting a state-supported church, while allowing each church to elect its own elders

1.18 Calvinists who wanted to remain separate from any other congregation, ruling themselves.

1.19 the keeping of all Anglicans and Presbyterians out of the House of Commons under Cromwell

1.20 nickname for Cromwell's troops

1.21 leader of the Roundheads who set himself up as military dictator after abolishing the monarchy

1.22 a. revolted against the Catholic Church, setting up the Church of England
b. accepted the Anglican Church as the state church and tolerated most religious groups, keeping disagreements under control
c. Anglican Church remained the state church, but the Puritan movement was getting very strong

1.23 Cromwell thoroughly trained his men in combat. The Cavaliers, on the other hand, were flashy, but poorly trained. Singing hymns and believing God was on their side, the Roundhead's faith and determination were too much for the Cavaliers.

1.24 Any order:
a. took over House of Commons, only allowing independent Calvinists to remain
b. abolished the House of Lords
c. abolished the monarchy, declaring himself military dictator

1.25 a. He was trustworthy, had a keen mind, was an excellent public speaker, and was an able statesman.
b. He dealt harshly with the people, crushing rebellions.

1.26 a. wanted the king to be merely a figurehead with the real power of government belonging to Parliament
b. wanted a strong hereditary king, but didn't want him to have absolute power

1.27 Charles II dealt carefully with Parliament. When opposed, he tried other means. James II cared nothing of what Parliament thought and was bold in his Catholicism and his divine right to rule.

1.28 a. Parliament did not want another Catholic king.
b. They were invited to rule by Parliament.
c. Mary was the daughter of James II.

1.29 b

1.30 b

1.31 d

1.32 a

1.33 c

1.34 b

1.35 b

1.36 Examples:
For Whig—I want to protect myself from being ruled by an overbearing monarch. I believe in the people having the upper voice in government; therefore, I want the real power to be held by Parliament, giving representation to all beliefs, not just Anglican.
For Tory—Although I do not want the king to have total power, I want a strong hereditary king to lead us. We need a strong, dominant figure of power to rule the country. I want the Anglican Church to be supreme in England, rather than these ever-changing Calvinists with their insubordinate ideas. Security and tradition are for me, not change.

1.37 a, c, d

1.38 a, b, d

1.39 a, b, c

1.40 a, b, c

1.41 a, b, d

1.42 The working class had little or no representation.

1.43 a. They are usually introduced in the king or queen's opening speech to Parliament.
b. They are passed in Parliament.
c. They are enforced by the prime minister and cabinet.

1.44 a. He heads the government and brings the monarch's ideas to Parliament.
b. when his party is no longer in the majority in the House of Commons
c. by the monarch's selection of a new prime minister
d. the recognized leader of the majority party in the House of Commons

SECTION TWO

2.1 a. Virginia
b. 1607

2.2 Writs of Assistance

2.3 Trade Acts

2.4 a. Englishmen
b. charters

2.5 d

2.6 a

2.7 b

2.8 a

2.9 Colonists were mainly English middle and lower classes, seeking economic betterment or religious freedom. They left to escape the continuous political upheaval, religious friction, or poor economic conditions.

2.10 They enforced the principle of mercantilism, discouraged buying and selling with foreign countries without English approval, insisted Americans ship goods only on English ships, allowed many products to only be sold in England, and demanded that goods from foreign countries being shipped to the United States be inspected and taxed in England first.

2.11 The colonists avoided the laws by smuggling and increasingly came into conflict with England over them.

2.12 Either order:
a. French
b. Indians
Either order:
c. English
d. colonists

2.13 a. General Wolfe
b. General Montcalm

2.14 Either order:
a. Canada
b. the land east of the Mississippi

2.15 Trade Laws

2.16 defense of the colonies

2.17 First Continental Congress

2.18 Boston Tea Party

2.19 Colonists moving west were checked and harassed by French who owned land beyond the Appalachian Mountains.

2.20 Many colonists refused to support the British troops, and many states only allowed their men to fight within the state. Colonists helped very little financially and continued trading with the French during the war.

2.21 Example:
I believe my rights as an Englishman are being horribly abused, with unfair taxation and trials without a jury, in addition to searches of my property without a warrant or warning. I believe the Trade Laws are unfair; therefore, I am showing my disgust at this treatment by dumping the tea which, too, is highly taxed.

2.22 true

2.23 false

2.24 false

2.25 true

2.26 true

2.27 true

2.28 false

2.29 false

2.30 AMERICA
Advantages
-fighting on home soil; protecting own homes; and good knowledge of the land
-leadership of Washington
Disadvantages
-greatly outnumbered at sea
-some state troops only allowed to fight within state
-Congress had little power; could not tax to raise support for the war
- militia had little organized training
ENGLAND
Advantages
- better organized and equipped on land and sea
-blockades by ships almost unchallenged
-well-trained, larger army
-backed financially
Disadvantages
-fought far from home
-had to transport equipment and men across the Atlantic
-unfamiliar with the geography of the land
-English citizens not totally behind the war effort
-had to hire Hessians to fight
-poor leadership

2.31 a. It was European tradition to discontinue military offensives during winter months.
b. They were able to attack the British by surprise at night in Trenton.
c. It gave them the incentive to keep on fighting in spite of their desperate winter circumstances.

2.32 teacher check

2.33 Lexington/Concord
a. Captain John Parker
b. Major John Pitcairn under General Gage
c. just defending their city; attempting to show they were serious
d. attempt to seize United States' war supplies
e. British/Americans
f. first battle of Revolution, beginning of actual fighting

Return March to Boston
a. no answer
b. Gage
c. used every means of concealment as they shot—trees, shrubs, and so on
d. none—were returning to Boston in a marching formation
e. Americans
f. aroused Americans' will to fight and showed new way of fighting

Battle of Trenton
a. Washington
b. no answer
c. crossed the Delaware at night–surprise attack
d. none—they were surprised
e. Americans
f. psychologically inspired Americans to keep fighting

Seizure of Seraphis
a. John Paul Jones
b. Captain Richard Pearson
c. after sighting Seraphis, pursued it, lined up with it side-by-side used guns, grenades, light cannons, some fighting, mostly perseverance
d. attempted to bring Jones' surrender with use of superior ship and artillery
e. Americans
f. inspired naval forces; greatly outnumbered

Battle of Yorktown
a. Washington
b. Cornwallis
c. Washington surrounded Yorktown with his army and a French army. The French fleet blocked the British ships from coming.
d. Marched to Yorktown to wait for the British fleet which was to arrive
e. Americans
f. brought Cornwallis' surrender and led to United States independence.

2.34 There was very little government until the Second Continental Congress received some centralized power, as outlined in the Articles of Confederation, only six months before Cornwallis' surrender.

2.35 They established a one-house congress which passed laws that had to be enforced by the individual states. Powers included making war, peace, borrowing money and settling state arguments.

2.36 He is elected by the electoral college, composed of electors chosen by the people, who traditionally vote for the candidate of their political party.

2.37 Executive
-chief executive heads the government
- President
Legislative
-makes the laws
-House of Representatives and Senate
Judicial
-interprets laws and evaluates how they apply
- district courts, courts of appeal, and Supreme Court

2.38 Example:
I would definitely stress the flexibility and enduring factor the amendments provide, and the automatic checking of power between the three branches of government, which keeps one from becoming too powerful. Also, I would point out how efficiently it meets the needs of the United States.

SECTION THREE

3.1 Any order:
a. the clergy
b. the nobles
c. middle and peasant classes

3.2 Any order:
a. Voltaire
b. Rousseau
c. Montesquieu

3.3 Any order:
a. equality of man
b. man's right to self-government
c. the fact that the colonies broke away from a king

3.4 King Louis XV was absolute monarch of France and exhibited a lazy and indifferent attitude to his people's needs, taking no steps to head off the coming revolution or to improve the national economy.

3.5 his laziness; the desperate financial situation in France which he took no steps to remedy; the inspiration of the victory of the United States over England that ended in self-government

3.6 Example:
I think we should have a voice in our government—I am tired of lazy kings who care little about our needs. I believe the tax situation is totally unfair, with poor people paying heavy taxes while the rich go free. The rich have too many special privileges. I am for equality of the people and representation of the people in government.

3.7 c

3.8 b

3.9 d

3.10 a

3.11 the former French legislative body, revived under Louis XVI

3.12 the new legislative body, born under Louis XVI, mainly third estate

3.13 the vow of the National Assembly to write a constitution

3.14 French Independence Day, when Paris mobs revolted against the king's army

3.15 the declaration adopted by the National Assembly, giving Frenchmen freedom of speech, press, religion, and other rights

3.16 When he rejected the financial proposals, French banks refused to lend him further money. Desperately, he recalled the French legislature to help him to solve the problem.

3.17 When the king wanted all three estates to meet separately, the third estate refused, declaring itself a National Assembly. Barred from the Estates General, they met and agreed to write a Constitution, whereupon the king let them get together. The National Assembly was born.

3.18 The Austrian and Prussian armies were in the process of invading France because of the takeover by Danton, who formed a new government. This new government was in danger of being conquered by foreign armies.

3.19 draft or conscript

3.20 Directory

3.21 consuls

3.22 Set up the committee of Public Safety which jailed and killed opponents of the government. It ended the monarchy, declaring France a republic and executing the kings . When their army met with success, they announced their intention of liberating all of Europe from the Old Regime. Later reforms were made in law and education, and the metric system was adopted.

3.23 It was unable to give France a stable government or peaceful existence because it was too weak; trying to please all the people, it pleased few. The Directors, instead of working in unity, constantly argued.

3.24 With many impressive military triumphs, he became a national hero. The French were restless for a strong leader. The Directory was extremely weak, so he forced three to resign, arrested two, dissolved the Parliament, and took over with his army and the people's support.

3.25 <u>Directory</u>
-five Directors
-none
-Together, the Directors were to control government.
-chose the Directors' Law-making branch
-weak because of Directors arguing; no one man in charge
<u>Consulate</u>
-three Consuls
-First Consul
-command of armed forces; power to appoint or dismiss officers; could oppose new laws
-little power; only puppets of First Consul
-as strong as First Consul, little voice for people

3.26 Example:
The Directory is extremely weak and is accomplishing little in providing me and my family with a stable government or peace. Our French armies are meeting defeat all around the world. We need one man, a strong and able leader, to get us out of this weakness or we may be overthrown. Napoleon has shown great military genius and strong leadership qualities. I think he can make a difference and bring peace and security back to France.

3.27 Coup D'Etat

3.28 November 9, 1799

3.29 Napoleonic Era

3.30 nationalism

3.31 the Code Napoleon

3.32 the Hundred Days War

3.33 a. empire
b. Emperor Napoleon I

3.34 b. Oath of the Tennis Court

3.35 c. defeated Syria

3.36 e. Code Napoleon

3.37 a. Portuguese revolt

3.38 Trying to overcome England, Napoleon's fleet failed, meeting disaster here. With defeat by England, England remained out of Napoleon's reach.

3.39 It began the series of events leading to Napoleon's defeat. The invasion left Napoleon's troops in shambles, and his decision to return to Europe led to his defeat.

3.40 In this battle against Austria, Russia, the English, and the Swedish, Napoleon met his defeat and was later forced to give up his throne.

3.41 After Napoleon's return, European nations met here to crush Napoleon's power once and for all, banishing him to St. Helena.

3.42 Frenchmen enjoyed a far greater amount of liberty and equality, a greater voice in government, and an outgrowth of free thinking.

SECTION ONE

1.1 b

1.2 f

1.3 e

1.4 a

1.5 c

1.6 c

1.7 d

1.8 d

1.9 b

1.10 e

1.11 a

1.12 d

1.13 a. provided greater heat when blasted with air
b. used to heat impurities from iron with great intensity
c. provided a lighter metal for more varied and efficient use

1.14 a. larger number of products produced
b. products were better quality
c. lower prices of products because of greater quantity produced

1.15 Kay's flying shuttle replaced hand weaving by machine, Hargreaves spinning jenny spun thread by machine, and Whitney's cotton gin separated cotton seeds from the lint. All three increased speed, efficiency, and production, allowing more to be produced at lowest cost and less manpower.

1.16 a, c, d

1.17 a, b, d

1.18 a, b, c

1.19 a, b, c

1.20 a, b, d

1.21 a, b, d

1.22 Machines became too large and expensive to keep at home; also needed water power to run these, so moved factories near water sources.

1.23 He could combine his assets with other businessmen to start one main business. Stockholders would supply the additional capital needed in exchange for a share of the profits.

1.24 Hint:
Once independent and doing the work I loved, now I need no skill, am bored, no longer independent. I'm really worth little, only do the same dull job day in, day out, not using any creativity.

1.25 true

1.26 true

1.27 true

1.28 false

1.29 true

1.30 false

1.31 c

1.32 a. able to power the machines; more versatile use of power
b. made road travel safer, more enjoyable, less delays
c. quicker distribution and cheaper transportation of goods
d. faster and safer than road travel; could carry much freight

1.33 Steam-powered factories did not have to be located near water sources. Steam power could power other machines, was a much more versatile power source, and was easily mobile.

SECTION TWO

2.1 true

2.2 true

2.3 false

2.4 false

2.5 true

2.6 deposits of coal and rivers and streams, plus favorable land and climate for agricultural industry

2.7 Hint:
I was encouraged by the achievements of industry in England in Europe, and taking into account the positive American climate for industry and the chance for making large profits, I gladly invested my capital, hoping to help make America wealthy, showing England we were as good as they or better.

2.8 f

2.9 h

2.10 g

2.11 b

2.12 d

2.13 a

2.14 c

2.15 true

2.16 false

2.17 false

2.18 true

2.19 true

2.20
a. iron plow, steel plow, reaper, thresher, cotton gin
b. reaper, thresher, cotton gin, sewing machine
c. Cumberland road, canals, steamboat, railroad
d. railroad

2.21
a. forced the United States to produce what she had gotten from England
b. safer, quicker, more enjoyable road travel
c. quicker distribution of goods-led to international boost in trade
d. improved speed of distribution, much more efficient transportation
e. cheaper transportation of goods, also sometimes quicker
f. replaced hand cutting and separating of grain

2.22 c

2.23 d

2.24 a

2.25 b

2.26 The strength and backing of Northern industry, continually supplying war equipment, and the immigrant staff allowed Northerners to go South to fight.

2.27 The demand for war equipment kept industry busy and profits high, increasing production. The soldiers' vacant jobs lowered unemployment.

2.28 Industry provided constant replacement of supplies. Also, transportation and communication methods greatly aided the movement of soldiers and supplies and the sending of messages.

2.29 false

2.30 true

2.31 false

2.32 true

2.33 true

2.34 fa1se

2.35 allowed broken parts to be replaced without replacing whole product

2.36 sped production and reduced cost per unit

2.37 provided a tougher, more versatile structural material and building material for factory equipment, transportation needs, and building construction

2.38 d

2.39 g

2.40 a

2.41 b

2.42 h

2.43 f

2.44 c

2.45 c

2.46 d

2.47 a

2.48 Hint:
Modern transportation made the spread of the Gospel possible to every part of the

world. The airplane is especially useful to missionaries in remote areas, such as jungles. Many Christian ministries carry on correspondence courses by mail or counseling by phone. Faster mail service—by plane—helps missionaries keep in touch with the home board and supporters, and quickens their receiving of supplies

2.49 e

2.50 d

2.51 a

2.52 b

2.53 c

2.54 h

2.55 f

2.56 c

2.57 d

2.58 a

2.59 Hint:
The Christian owner would not use illegal means to combat competition; neither would he allow his firm to sell inferior goods for higher prices. He would conform to government regulations in accordance to obeying the Scriptures and make working conditions satisfactory for his workers. His main goal in everything would be to glorify Christ, not to gain riches.

2.60 teacher check

SECTION THREE

3.1 c

3.2 a

3.3 d

3.4 c

3.5 Hint:
Once I was my own boss, providing the food, housing, and clothing my family needs. I did the kind of work I enjoyed, now I'm dependent on my factory for everything. We live in a bad neighborhood and I feel worthless. Obviously, I made a mistake—I should have stayed on the farm, at least until working and housing conditions changed.

3.6 For socialists—socialism equalizes people, protecting people who are creative or ambitious. It is less fluctuating than the free enterprise system—more inflexible. It also helps to equalize the wealth, and is advantageous to the extremely poor. The free enterprise system is ideal for the creative and ambitious. Ideas are not stifled. It rewards hard work, therefore the goals are almost limitless. It is also not controlled by government.

3.7 false

3.8 true

3.9 true

3.10 true

3.11 false

3.12 true

3.13 true

3.14 The employee is instructed in Hebrews 13:17, 1 Pet. 2:18, Ephesians 6:5-8, Col. 3:22, and Titus 2:9 to be obedient to his employer whether he is just or unjust or doing service to God and not to man. Employers are instructed in Ephesians 6:9 and Col. 4:1 to not threaten their employees, but to be just and equal in their dealings with others.

3.15 standard of living

3.16 demand

3.17 a. better communication
b. cheaper transportation

3.18 a. export
b. import

3.19 tariffs

3.20 international cooperation

3.21 by passing labor laws democratically, through the organization of labor unions that used collective bargaining, or by compromising; discussing peaceably

3.22 The world's economy has been raised immensely, increasing the world's standard of living to a relatively prosperous level in comparison to a century ago.

3.23 Nations depend on other countries to buy their surplus goods so that they in turn can buy the products and raw materials they need.

3.24 The new transportation methods made distribution of goods quicker, safer, and more economical, in turn making the availability of products greater.

3.25 The few roads were in horrible condition. Bandits were abundant on land and sea, making trade difficult and unprofitable. An added expense was the high taxes charged to use roads.

3.26
a. made land travel quicker, safer, more enjoyable
b. made distribution cheaper and easier, travel more convenient
c. quickened distribution, lowered transportation costs on water
d. made distribution quicker, cheaper, and easier on land

SECTION ONE

1.1 c

1.2 g

1.3 a

1.4 h

1.5 b

1.6 d

1.7 e

1.8 a. Avantages
Positive national spirit brings unity to a country, pride in one's heritage, and willingness to fight in time of war.
b. Brings raw materials for industry and wealth to a national economy. Also, colonization sets up better defense of nation around the world.
c. Provides defense of a nation during war times. Also increases production of industry and lowers unemployment.
Disadvantages
a. Extreme nationalism disrupts negotiations on a peaceful basis as every nation wants its way. Leads to conflict, even war.
b. Causes clashes over desirable areas leading to war. Stifles independence of the area colonized.
c. When done to extremes, a nation becomes so military-minded that war becomes almost sought.

1.9 true

1.10 true

1.11 false

1.12 true

1.13 false

1.14 true

1.15 teacher check

1.16 Alliance
a. 1. Triple Alliance
b. 1. Triple Alliance
c. 1. Triple Entente
d. 1. Triple Entente
e. 1. Triple Entente (Allies)
f. 1. Triple Entente
g. 1. Triple Alliance

Reasons for Entrance
a. 2. when ultimatum to Serbia was rejected, declared war on Serbia for assassination of Ferdinand; anti-Austrian movement
b. 2. on the basis of the Triple Alliance, joined sides with Austria against Russia; Russia ignored Germany's demand that Russia cease mobilization
c. 2. armed to defend Serbia against Alliance; when Germany declared war, they counteracted.
d. 2. German violation of Belgian neutrality
e. 2. joined Entente in accordance with previous treaty with Britain in 1902
f. 2. involved in war between Germany and Russia; thus Germany declared war on France
g. 2. joined Allies because of desire for Austrian-held territory

1.17 United States

1.18 Russia

1.19 Chateau-Thierry

1.20 Bolshevik Party

1.21 c

1.22 d

1.23 c

1.24 Location
a. Belgium and France (almost to Paris)
b. France
c. Chateau-Thierry, France
d. began at Cantigny through France and Belgium

Strategy
a. Planned to bring French surrender quickly before Russia was fully prepared to attack so they would not have war on both fronts at once
b. Combined German army staged massive French attack to defeat France before Americans entered the war
c. Allied troops and fresh American troops held off the previously successful German advance
d. To drive Germans back out of France and Belgium and force German surrender

Victor
- a. Germany won many victories early in the offensive. Then France drove the Germans back.
- b. Victory for Germans until Chateau-Thierry
- c. Allies held German advance
- d. Allies

SECTION TWO

2.1 c

2.2 d

2.3 e

2.4 a

2.5 e

2.6 c

2.7 a

2.8 d

2.9 c

2.10 b

2.11 c

2.12 a. A just peace would limit bitterness and restore Europe to a healthy economic condition, preventing another world war. Wilson felt harsh treatment would result in growing tensions and bitterness.
b. Advocates of a harsh peace thought German rise to power would be prevented only by division, disarmament, and firm discipline, crippling Germany so much they could not rise again.

2.13 false

2.14 true

2.15 false

2.16 true

2.17 true

2.18 true

2.19 a. Americans resented their involvement in the First World War and feared that involvement in the League might lead them into more world involvement and another war.
b. Without American support, the League lacked the strength it needed to enforce its policies and took away a lot of the confidence other nations had placed in it.

2.20 Hint:
Matthew 11:28 offers relief from the heavy burdens of life; Matthew 6:25-34 implores the Christian to refrain from worrying about his economic situation knowing the Lord will take care of him; I Peter 5:7 assures the Christian of Christ's care, and Philippians 4:4, 11, 13, and 19 teaches us to rejoice always, being content in every state, knowing that God will supply all our needs.

2.21 c

2 22 f

2.23 b

2.24 a

2.25 g

2.26 h

2.27 e

2.28 true

2.29 false

2.30 true

2.31 true

2.32 true

2.33 Military build-up increases industrial production with the demand for war equipment and supplies, thus raising the economy and reducing unemployment with the added jobs of industry.

2.34 Haile Selassie

2.35 League of Nations

2.36 Treaty of Versailles

2.37 Russia

2.38 Poland

2.39 b

2.40 c

2.41 d

SECTION THREE

3.1 d

3.2 e

3.3 g

3.4 f

3.5 h

3.6 a

3.7 i

3.8 b

3.9 false

3.10 true

3.11 true

3.12 true

3.13 false

3.14 true

3.15 true

3.16 true

3.17 false

3.18 true

3.19 The Allies drove Rommel from Africa while Russia counterattacked Germany. Next, they drove up the Italian peninsula. Then, after the Normandy invasion, they drove across France and Belgium, and while Russia closed in from the east, the Allies drove from the west and the Russians brought the German surrender in Berlin.

3.20 Pacific

3.21 Douglas MacArthur

3.22 marines

3.23 Doolittle

3.24 Either order:
a. Philippine Sea
b. Leyte Gulf

3.25 kamikaze

3.26 Either order:
a. Nagasaki
b. Hiroshima

3.27 d

3.28 d

3.29 c

3.30 Hints:

a. The alternate land invasion of Japan would bring a much greater proposed loss of life than the bombings. It was successful in bringing the Japanese surrender.

b. Thousands of lives were lost, and no one will ever be able to prove that there would have been more lives lost in an invasion: The Japanese may have surrendered at the invasions of the homeland.

3.31 Hint:
Deuteronomy 32:35-36 and Hebrews 10:30 teach that vengeance belongs to the Lord, not us. He will judge wrongs in His own time. We are to show love to our brothers and fellow man, and forgive (Ephesians 4:32) them as God has forgiven us.

3.32 United States President during World War II

3.33 British Prime Minister during World War II

3.34 Russian premier—World War II spreading his communist dogma

3.35 document stating democratic goals for World War II of Britain and America

3.36 organization for world peace settlements following World War II

3.37 new nation formed from occupation zones of the democratic nations—America, Britain, France—after World War II

3.38 nation formed from communist occupation

3.39 c

3.40 b

3.41 d

3.42 a. a
b. b

3.43 b

3.44 Hint:
There can be no lasting peace until the Prince of Peace, Jesus Christ, (Isaiah 9:6) is in control on earth, at which time (Isaiah 9:7) there shall be no end to His peace.

3.45 Members
a. 1. represented by delegates of all other nations
b. 1. 11 members— U.S., Britain, France, Russia, China, and six others elected every two years
c. 1. clerics, administrators, advisors
d. 1. one, elected by General Assembly every 5 years
e. 1. 15 judges appointed by the General Assembly and Security Council

Duties
a. 2. discusses problems, recommends action, elects Secretary-General and judges
b. 2. maintains peace, settles disputes, curbs aggressive action
c. 2. full-time cleric, administration and advisory duties
d. 2. reports United Nations business to General Assembly, attends all UN meetings, makes recommendations to Security Council
e. 2. settles national disputes brought before them

3.46 false

3.47 false

3.48 true

3.49 false

3.50 true

3.51 false

3.52 true

3.53 Hints:
It was based on the positive policy of settling world disagreements peacefully rather than war. It has checkmates, especially in Security Council, to prevent hasty action. Forum allows each nation to voice its opinions.

Weaknesses
-Security Council action easily vetoed
-equal power to smaller and larger nations
-financial dependence on United States
-free nations do not always band together against communism
-only as strong as its members obey

Solutions
-two must veto or a majority
-power representative of population
-spread the financial burden proportionally
-free nations need to unite to fight aggression
-more muscle, regulations put into rules—if nations do not respond, withdraw them

3.54 teacher check

SECTION ONE

1.1 a. the fall of communism in Eastern Europe, 1989
b. the breakup of the Soviet Union, 1991

1.2 (Wording will vary) The United States was committed to keeping communism in the places where it already existed. The U.S. would oppose its spread anywhere else in the world.

1.3 Any order:
a. United States
b. Union of Soviet Socialist Republics (USSR)– *Not* Russia

1.4 Any order:
a. Poland
b. Hungary
c. Czecholsovakia
d. Bulgaria
e. Romania

1.5 The U.S. expected a period of post-war cooperation with the Soviets that could be used to convince them to leave Eastern Europe.

1.6 a. Albania
b. Yugoslavia

1.7 false

1.8 true

1.9 false

1.10 false

1.11 true

1.12 Teacher check: Answers may include:
Weaknesses: lack of enforcement, sheer size, veto power
Strengths: large participation, prestige, public debate of issues

1.13 the Soviet Union

1.14 NATO

1.15 Marshall Plan

1.16 the Nationalists and Communists

1.17 Mao Zedong

1.18 The Communists had control of north China, and the Soviet captured Japanese supplies. The peasants were tired of corrupt government and supported Mao. The Nationalists did not receive much American aid.

1.19 He publicly opposed the decision of his commander-in-chief.

1.20 a. China became communist
b. Soviets exploded their first nuclear bomb

1.21 Both sides possessed massive nuclear arsenals which might destroy the world if they were used.

1.22 They began airlifting supplies to the city.

1.23 Repatriation: Many communist prisoners of war did not want to go home. The communists insisted on mandatory return of all prisoners. The allies refused.

1.24 Communism was contained in North Korea and did not spread further.

1.25 He sent a landing force to Inchon halfway up the Korean Peninsula. These troops cut off the North Korean troops assaulting the Pusan Perimeter and freed Seoul.

1.26 true

1.27 true

1.28 false

1.29 true

1.30 The U-2 Incident: An American spy plane was shot down over the Soviet Union.

1.31 a. Great Britain
b. France
c. Israel

1.32 to prevent East Germans from fleeing to the West through Berlin

1.33 Cuban exiles, trained by the United States, attempted an invasion to overthrow Castro. President Kennedy refused to give them air cover and the attempt failed.

1.34 to prevent the delivery of nuclear missiles from the Soviet Union.

1.35 The Hungarian people revolted and put in a reform government.

1.36 d

1.37 b

1.38 c

1.39 e

1.40 a

1.41 e

1.42 b

1.43 a

1.44 f

1.45 d

1.46 c

1.47 limited

1.48 Gulf of Tonkin Resolution

1.49 Ho Chi Minh City

1.50 American Congress

1.51 Tet Offensive

1.52 the first free trade union in a communist country

1.53 a reform movement in Czechoslovakia; it was ended by an invasion by the Warsaw Pact

1.54 It began the opening up of China, but cut the United States off from long time ally, Taiwan.

1.55 to support a communist coup there

1.56 by stopping grain sales to the Soviet Union and boycotting the Olympics in Moscow

1.57 a period of better relations between the super powers in the 1970s

1.58 The Polish government declared martial law, arrested the leaders, and eventually outlawed the group.

1.59 Strategic Arms Limitation Treaty; it cut the number of nuclear weapons held by the superpowers.

1.60 glasnost; perestroika

1.61 Vaclav Havel

1.62 Romania

1.63 Yugoslavia

1.64 Berlin Wall

1.65 leaving to go to West Germany

1.66 false

1.67 true

1.68 true

1.69 false

1.70 false

1.71 Boris Yeltsin

1.72 three

1.73 unemployment, crime, and lack of knowledge about business

1.74 Boris Yeltsin

1.75 The people took to the streets to oppose it and much of the army did not support it.

1.76 Commonwealth of Independent Nations

1.77 teacher check

1.78 teacher check

SECTION TWO

2.1 Isthmus of Panama

2.2 Mount McKinley

2.3 a. Superior
b. Michigan
c. Huron
d. Erie
e. Ontario

2.4 is

2.5 Mississippi

2.6 a. Rocky Mountains
b. Sierra Madre

2.7 United States

2.8 Institutional Revolutionary Party (PRI)

2.9 Canada

2.10 Kalaallit Nunaat

2.11 deficit

2.12 NAFTA

2.13 d

2.14 c

2.15 b

2.16 h

2.17 g

2.18 a

2.19 e

2.20 f

2.21 Cuba was a very aggressive communist nation, sending troops to support "revolutions" all over the world. It was also economically dependent upon the Soviet Union.

2.22 Cuba remained communist but lost its subsidies from the Soviet Union. The economy was severely damaged.

2.23 Haiti is a very poor country which has often been ruled by dictators. The cycle of poverty will be difficult to change. It will also be a challenge for the country to remain a democracy.

2.24 Teacher check. Student should discuss the problems of supporting a military government just because it is anti-communist.

2.25 Andes

2.26 Amazon River

2.27 Spanish

2.28 Angel Falls

2.29 fourth

2.30 f

2.31 c

2.32 g

2.33 d

2.34 a

2.35 e

2.36 h

2.37 b

2.38 a capitalist democracy allied with the United States, usually in the western part of Europe

2.39 France, Switzerland, Italy, Austria, Germany, and Slovenia

2.40 It is surrounded by oceans on three sides, and the Gulf Stream circulates warm Caribbean water up to it.

2.41 begins in Germany and flows into Austria, through Budapest, Hungary, into Croatia, Yugoslavia, Romania, Bulgaria, and into the Black Sea along the border of Romania and the Ukraine

2.42 the Ural Mountains, Ural River, and the Caspian Sea

2.43 a. Mount El'brus
b. Russia

2.44 a. Volga
b. Russia

2.45 They are not part of the European Union.

2.46 (any order) Belgium, Liechtenstein, Luxembourg, Netherlands, Norway, Spain, Sweden, United Kingdom

2.47 live, work, and vote

2.48 They cost too much to maintain in the less robust economies since the 1970s.

2.49 a. European Coal and Steel Community—1951
b. European Economic Community—1957
c. European Atomic Energy Commission—1957
d. European Community—1967

2.50 capitalist democracies

2.51 a. Belarus
b. Estonia
c. Kazakhstan
d. Latvia
e. Lithuania
f. Russia
g. Slovenia
h. Ukraine

2.52 a. Albania
b. Hungary
c. Romania
d. Poland

2.53 The economies are based on state ownership of everything, people do not know how to run businesses, and they produce low-quality goods. Unemployment and crime are high.

2.54 a. Serbs
b. Croats
c. Muslims

2.55 They peacefully divided their nation into Slovakia and the Czech Republic.

2.56 a. ethnic disputes
b. no tradition of democratic government
c. corruption
d. dominance of former communists

2.57 a. Estonia
b. Latvia
c. Lithuania

2.58 spiritual renewal and Christians who are salt and light

2.59 Sahara

2.60 equator

2.61 Ithmus of Suez

2.62 Savanna

2.63 Straight of Gibraltar

2.64 Nile

2.65 rain forest

2.66 through east Africa from the Red Sea to Mozambique

2.67 Mount Kilimanjaro

2.68 Atlas

2.69 Islam (Muslim)

2.70 South Africa

2.71 a. massacres
b. famines

2.72 a. military
b. one-party dictatorships

2.73 a. Great Britain
b. France

2.74 Islamic fundamentalists who want to force the government to enforce Islamic laws and customs

2.75 They divided the continent up without regard to the location of the ethnic groups. Nations are now made up of different groups who have no loyalty to each other and are culturally different.

2.76 Pamir Knot

2.77 a. Himalaya
b. Kunlun

2.78 largest

2.79 a. Tigris
b. Euphrates

2.80 a. Huang
b. Chang

2.81 Gobi

2.82 Mount Everest

2.83 Arabian Peninsula

2.84 g

2.85 b

2.86 d

2.87 a

2.88 f

2.89 c

2.90 e

2.91 They divided the nation and created Pakistan for the Muslims. Millions of Muslims fled into Pakistan and millions of Hindus fled out of it; thousands died in fighting along the way.

2.92 They were Cambodian communists. They were very brutal, emptying cities to force people to work in the country. Over a million people were murdered or died of starvation.

2.93 Any order:
a. Thailand
b. Brunei
c. Indonesia
d. Malaysia
e. Singapore
f. Philippines

2.94 Any order:
a. Russia
b. Kazakhstan
c. Ubekistan
d. Turkmenistan
e. Kyrgyzstan
f. Tajikistan
g. Azerbaijan
h. Armenia
i. Georgia

2.95 to create a classless society

2.96 Universities, businesses, and even some government offices were attacked and closed by radical "Red Guards." The army had to be called in to quell the disturbances.

2.97 The government has remained dictatorial but has reformed the economy so that it is booming.

2.98 a. China
b. North Korea

2.99 Mao wanted to make China into an industrial nation in a few years and everything was accelerated to reach this goal.

2.100 a. China
b. North Korea

2.101 Queen Elizabeth II of England

2.102 smallest

2.103 ANZUS

2.104 Indian Ocean

2.105 Great Barrier Reef

2.106 a. Simpson
b. Great Sandy
c. Gibson
d. Great Victoria

2.107 teacher check

SECTION ONE

1.1 Old Testament
1.2 Promised Land
1.3 captivity or Babylon
1.4 Abraham
1.5 Diaspora
1.6 true
1.7 false
1.8 true
1.9 true
1.10 false
1.11 Either order:
a. copper
b. tin
1.12 Either order:
a. horse
b. chariot
1.13 Any order:
a. calendar
b. irrigation system
c. written communication
d. government
1.14 pharaohs
1.15 false
1.16 true
1.17 false
1.18 true
1.19 false
1.20 false
1.21 false
1.22 teacher check
1.23 Because of poor soil, they could not raise the food they needed.
1.24 a blind Greek poet, author of the *Iliad* and the *Odyssey*
1.25 Crete
1.26 He failed to choose a successor himself.
1.27 Either order:
a. Athens
b. Sparta
1.28 lower
1.29 Augustus
1.30 citizenship
1.31 Julius Caesar
1.32 Diocletian
1.33 Roman Peace
1.34 provinces
1.35 Etruscans
1.36 It was attacked by Germanic tribes and could not defend itself; common people were impoverished; the government was corrupt; leaders were weak.
1.37 false
1.38 true
1.39 false
1.40 true
1.41 false
1.42 true
1.43 France
1.44 Vikings
1.45 breakup of the Roman Empire
1.46 Iberian
1.47 Huns
1.48 d
1.49 c
1.50 f
1.51 e
1.52 a
1.53 feudal system
1.54 the king
1.55 land granted to a lesser noble by a noble
1.56 peasants
1.57 money, soldiers, and equipment in time of war
1.58 William the Conqueror
1.59 c
1.60 d
1.61 a

1.62 b

1.63 c

1.64 a

1.65 true

1.66 false

1.67 true

1.68 false

1.69 true

1.70 false

1.71 to recapture the Holy Land and Jerusalem

1.72 They stimulated trade and the rise of towns and cities.

1.73 They had no monasteries and traveled from place to place.

1.74 Any order:
a. preserving ancient manuscripts
b. taught methods of agriculture
c. cared for the poor and sick

1.75 Jerusalem

SECTION TWO

2.1 Any order:
a. Rome
b. Venice
c. Milan
d. Florence
e. Genoa

2.2 Either order:
a. France
b. England

2.3 Florence

2.4 Joan of Arc

2.5 rebirth

2.6 false

2.7 true

2.8 true

2.9 false

2.10 true

2.11 j

2.12 i

2.13 a

2.14 k

2.15 b

2.16 c

2.17 f

2.18 g

2.19 e

2.20 h

2.21 Any order:
a. Romanesque
b. Gothic
c. Byzantine

2.22 proof

2.23 Leonardo da Vinci

2.24 Copernicus

2.25 gravity

2.26 b

2.27 d

2.28 a

2.29 d

2.30 c

2.31 a

2.32 b

2.33 false

2.34 false

2.35 true

2.36 true

2.37 false

2.38 true

2.39 Jesuits

2.40 Loyola

2.41 She had no sons to become heirs to the throne.

2.42 Anglican

2.43 reform

2.44 Ximenez
2.45 Act of Supremacy
2.46 false
2.47 false
2.48 true
2.49 true
2.50 false
2.51 divine right theory
2.52 War of the Roses
2.53 Henry VIII
2.54 a fleet of 130 Spanish ships sent by Philip II to attack England
2.55 It was nearly destroyed in battle and in storms.
2.56 Any order:
a. He resented England's interference in the Netherlands.
b. He wanted England to return to Catholicism.
c. He wanted to stop English interference in New World trade.
2.57 a Catholic extremist who tried to blow up the king and Parliament
2.58 f
2.59 c
2.60 a
2.61 d
2.62 g
2.63 e
2.64 Either order:
a. to make the king all-powerful in France
b. to make France supreme in Europe
2.65 Edict of Nantes
2.66 eight
2.67 sun
2.68 Either order:
a. wars
b. religious intolerance
2.69 money
2.70 false
2.71 false
2.72 true
2.73 true
2.74 false
2.75 true
2.76 true
2.77 true
2.78 d
2.79 f
2.80 a
2.81 g
2.82 e
2.83 b

SECTION THREE

3.1 Any order:
 a. Thomas Jefferson
 b. Benjamin Franklin
 c. John Adams
 d. Robert Livingston
 e. Roger Sherman

3.2 Second Continental Congress

3.3 It declared the United States independent from England.

3.4 France

3.5 Articles of Confederation

3.6 George Washington

3.7 Either order:
 a. Congress had no power to issue taxes.
 b. Laws passed by Congress were left to the states to enforce.

3.8 c

3.9 a

3.10 c

3.11 d

3.12 b

3.13 b

3.14 d

3.15 a

3.16 f

3.17 c

3.18 a

3.19 b

3.20 d

3.21 g

3.22 England

3.23 Clayton Antitrust Act

3.24 capital

3.25 labor unions

3.26 true

3.27 false

3.28 false

3.29 true

3.30 false

3.31 true

3.32 true

3.33 United States

3.34 Russia

3.35 Either order:
 a. Europe
 b. the Pacific

3.36 Harry S. Truman

3.37 Poland

3.38 Pearl Harbor

3.39 Ethiopia

3.40 General Douglas MacArthur

3.41 It maintains peace, settles disputes and stops aggression by military means, if necessary.

3.42 all permanent employees of the United Nations

3.43 It is composed of fifteen judges appointed by the Security Council and General Assembly. They settle disputes between governments.

3.44 The General Assembly acts as a forum where views are expressed and policies are recommended.

3.45 Nuclear Arms

3.46 a. 1989
 b. 1991

3.47 Berlin Wall

3.48 Mikhail Gorbachev

3.49 Any order:
 a. Korea
 b. Afghanistan

3.50 Any order:
 a. China
 b. Vietnam
 c. Cuba

3.51 true

3.52 false

3.53 true

3.54 false

3.55 true

3.56 false

3.57 false

3.58 false

SELF TEST 1

1.01 j
1.02 e
1.03 h
1.04 a
1.05 c
1.06 b
1.07 d
1.08 f
1.09 i
1.010 k
1.011 c
1.012 d
1.013 a
1.014 b
1.015 d
1.016 a
1.017 c
1.018 a
1.019 b
1.020 b
1.021 true
1.022 false
1.023 true
1.024 false
1.025 false
1.026 true
1.027 true
1.028 false
1.029 true
1.030 true
1.031 evolution
1.032 thousand
1.033 sixth
1.034 Third
1.035 writing
1.036 animals or every living thing
1.037 Flood
1.038 farmland
1.039 Sumer
1.040 political

SELF TEST 2

2.01 i
2.02 h
2.03 a
2.04 c
2.05 b
2.06 d
2.07 e
2.08 f
2.09 g
2.010 k
2.011 b
2.012 a
2.013 d
2.014 c
2.015 b
2.016 a
2.017 d
2.018 c
2.019 d
2.020 b
2.021 false
2.022 true
2.023 false
2.024 true
2.025 false
2.026 true
2.027 true
2.028 true
2.029 true
2.030 false
2.031 embalming
2.032 three
2.033 writing or script
2.034 polytheism
2.035 Moses
2.036 vizier
2.037 army
2.038 gods
2.039 Rosetta
2.040 papyrus

SELF TEST 3

3.01 c
3.02 f
3.03 i
3.04 a
3.05 d
3.06 e
3.07 k
3.08 b
3.09 h
3.010 j
3.011 true
3.012 false
3.013 true
3.014 true
3.015 true
3.016 false
3.017 false
3.018 true
3.019 false
3.020 true
3.021 Egypt
3.022 iron
3.023 god
3.024 texts or books or writings
3.025 Israel
3.026 clay
3.027 man
3.028 282
3.029 Jerusalem
3.030 Jeremiah

SELF TEST 4

4.01 a
4.02 d
4.03 k
4.04 g
4.05 h
4.06 b
4.07 c
4.08 e
4.09 f
4.010 j
4.011 Flood
4.012 Noah
4.013 agriculture
4.014 pyramids
4.015 death
4.016 Abraham
4.017 Egypt
4.018 Moses
4.019 prime minister or chief justice or treasurer
4.020 Zoroaster
4.021 d
4.022 b
4.023 a
4.024 c
4.025 b
4.026 a
4.027 c
4.028 c
4.029 b
4.030 a

SELF TEST 1

1.01 f
1.02 a
1.03 i
1.04 c
1.05 k
1.06 g
1.07 b
1.08 e
1.09 h
1.010 j
1.011 India
1.012 caste
1.013 Shang
1.014 Sanskrit
1.015 God
1.016 Buddha
1.017 Hindu
1.018 Chinese
1.019 mountains
1.020 Confucius
1.021 true
1.022 true
1.023 false
1.024 true
1.025 false
1.026 false
1.027 true
1.028 true
1.029 false
1.030 true
1.031 It does not require the existence of a god.
1.032 Any order:
a. birth
b. sickness
or old age, death, despair
1.033 several major dynasties
1.034 a 200-year period of peace
1.035 in their art

SELF TEST 2

2.01 g
2.02 j
2.03 a
2.04 i
2.05 k
2.06 d
2.07 b
2.08 c
2.09 e
2.010 h
2.011 b
2.012 d
2.013 a
2.014 c
2.015 a
2.016 b
2.017 d
2.018 a
2.019 d
2.020 a
2.021 democracy
2.022 Athens, or Greece
2.023 despot
2.024 Marathon
2.025 Pericles
2.026 Parthenon
2.027 Sparta
2.028 philosopher
2.029 plague
2.030 Syracuse
2.031 false
2.032 false
2.033 true
2.034 true
2.035 false
2.036 true

2.037 true
2.038 true
2.039 false
2.040 false
2.041 Demosthenes
2.042 Greek
2.043 He reasoned his conclusion.
2.044 the atom
2.045 philosopher-kings

SELF TEST 3

3.01 false
3.02 true
3.03 false
3.04 false
3.05 true
3.06 false
3.07 true
3.08 true
3.09 true
3.010 true
3.011 true
3.012 false
3.013 true
3.014 false
3.015 false
3.016 v
3.017 k
3.018 i
3.019 c
3.020 s
3.021 b
3.022 m
3.023 r
3.024 g
3.025 d
3.026 o
3.027 q
3.028 p
3.029 f
3.030 l
3.031 n
3.032 e
3.033 a
3.034 t
3.035 j
3.036 youth
3.037 Alexander the Great
3.038 Latins
3.039 patricians
3.040 plebeians
3.041 Greeks
3.042 Virgil
3.043 Punic
3.044 Hannibal
3.045 dictator
3.046 the father of Christian monasticism
3.047 Either order:
a. taxation
b. price controls
3.048 regular clergy
3.049 Example: and the Father were not coequal or Christ and the Father were not of the same essence or nature)
3.050 Example: who fight for money rather than for a cause
3.051 Example: an archbishop who ruled a province of the Roman Church
3.052 a Latin translation of the Bible from the Hebrew and Greek texts done by St. Jerome
3.053 d
3.054 b
3.055 c
3.056 b
3.057 d
3.058 c
3.059 d
3.060 b
3.061 d
3.062 the Republic
3.063 one that is won at too great a cost
3.064 an ideal or perfect society
3.065 Greek
3.066 Example: The Nicene Creed was a formal statement of the church's belief in the Trinity as God in three Persons with Father, Son, and Spirit all being coequal.
3.067 Examples: main divisions: clergy and laity. Laity- all the faithful. Clergy — all priestly functions. Clergy — secular clergy and regular clergy. Secular — priest, bishop, archbishop or metropolitan, patriarch, did not take vows or belong to religious order. Regular clergy — hermits or monks, lived by a rule.
3.068 establishing the first monastic orders of the East

SELF TEST 1

1.01 false
1.02 true
1.03 false
1.04 false
1.05 true
1.06 false
1.07 true
1.08 true
1.09 g
1.010 f
1.011 c
1.012 b
1.013 e
1.014 a
1.015 Any order:
- a. Saxons
- b. Goths
- c. Vandals
- d. Angles
- e. Franks

1.016 Theodoric
1.017 Any order:
- a. oath-swearing
- b. compensation
- c. trial by ordeal (or combat)

1.018 Ravenna
1.019 Sutton Hoo burial ship
1.020 Vortigern
1.021 Byzantine
1.022 Clovis
1.023 Examples: witan, comitatus justice system, some Roman influence
1.024 Example: established Frankish kingdom, championed Roman Christianity, established Christianity in western Europe
1.025 *Beowulf*

SELF TEST 2

2.01 d
2.02 a
2.03 k
2.04 h
2.05 b
2.06 i
2.07 f
2.08 c
2.09 j
2.010 g
2.011 a
2.012 b
2.013 c
2.014 b
2.015 a
2.016 a
2.017 b
2.018 c
2.019 false
2.020 true
2.021 true
2.022 false
2.023 false
2.024 true
2.025 true
2.026 true
2.027 the emperor's personal guard
2.028 papa or pope
2.029 Asiatic
2.030 Examples:
- a. push westward by Huns
- b. the number of barbarians in the empire
- c. the weakened state of Roman military power

2.031 the site of Benedict's monastery
2.032
- a. Clovis
- b. Franks

2.033 relationship between Germanic leaders and their nobles (warriors) in which the warriors swore complete allegiance to the king or leader. The leader, in turn, took care of the needs of his warriors, including payment of debts.

2.034 Examples: need for land and grazing areas, nomadic tribes moving north, Muhammad strong religious and political leader, Islam provided reason for conquest - convert the infidels

2.035 Hint: Answer should include the Carolingian Renaissance was the period of time during Charlemagne's reign when schools were established, scholars were sought out to teach, classics were preserved, illuminated manuscripts were produced, and Alcuin was brought from England.

SELF TEST 3

3.01 false

3.02 true

3.03 true

3.04 false

3.05 true

3.06 false

3.07 false

3.08 true

3.09 true

3.010 true

3.011 d

3.012 g

3.013 a

3.014 j

3.015 f

3.016 b

3.017 h

3.018 e

3.019 c

3.020 subinfeudation

3.021 investiture

3.022 a. page
b. squire

3.023 a. apprentice
b. journeyman

3.024 Either order; examples:
a. Bologna
b. Paris

3.025 Any order:
a. music
b. geometry
c. arithmetic
d. astronomy

3.026 *The Canterbury Tales*

3.027 Either order:
a. Romanesque
b. Gothic

3.028 Paris

3.029 a. Hastings
b. William
c. 1066

3.030 too concerned with conquest of Italy and with being emperors

3.031 a. France and England
b. France

3.032 Christian Spanish movement to reconquer Spain from the Muslims lasted nearly 400 years

3.033 Any order:
a. baptism
b. confirmation
c. penance
d. Holy Eucharist
e. matrimony
f. holy orders
g. extreme unction

3.034 Christian military expeditions to the Holy Land and the East to win back Holy Land from the "infidels"

3.035 Examples: major figures and developments: Figures: Anthony of Egypt, Basil, Benedict, Jerome, Gregory the Great, Bernard of Clairvaux, Francie, Dominic Developments: hermit- monastery-lived by rule-took vows- promoted learning- established schools- hosptials- spread Christianity as teachers and missionaries

SELF TEST 1

1.01 false
1.02 true
1.03 true
1.04 false
1.05 true
1.06 false
1.07 true
1.08 true
1.09 true
1.010 true
1.011 Bertrand du Guesclin
1.012 Flanders
1.013 a. English
b. French
1.014 de' Medici
1.015 florin
1.016 a. Lancasters
b. Yorks
c. a claim to the English throne
1.017 painter
1.018 Any order:
a. Michelangelo
b. Raphael
c. da Vinci
1.019 g
1.020 a
1.021 b
1.022 c
1.023 f
1.024 d
1.025 e
1.026 i
1.027 Copernicus's theory that the universe centered around the sun
1.028 a form of government in which only the privileged few had the power
1.029 a medieval form of architecture utilizing low arches and thick walls
1.030 paid professional soldiers
1.031 a church court which investigated, tried, and convicted heretics
1.032 a period of transition or change bridging medieval times and modern
1.033 Any order:
a. growth of trade and wealth
b. rise of middle class
c. decline of feudalism
d. the return to early Greek and Roman ideas
1.034 Any order:
a. government
b. the arts and architecture
c. literature and thought
d. science

SELF TEST 2

2.01 false
2.02 true
2.03 false
2.04 false
2.05 true
2.06 true
2.07 true
2.08 true
2.09 false
2.010 false
2.011 true
2.012 false
2.013 Any order:
a. government
b. the arts
c. literature and thought
d. science
2.014 Bertrand du Guesclin
2.015 a. Henry VII
b. England
2.016 Nicolaus Copernicus

2.017 Any order:
a. Galileo
b. Kepler
c. Newton

2.018 John Calvin

2.019 Anabaptists

2.020 ninety-five theses

2.021 nepotism

2.022 Lollards

2.023 Gustavus II

2.024 d

2.025 a

2.026 f

2.027 g

2.028 b

2.029 e

2.030 i

2.031 c

2.032 m

2.033 k

2.034 j

2.035 l

2.036 d

2.037 c

2.038 b

2.039 b

2.040 Example:
It was both political and religious in nature. Henry VIII established the Anglican Church so that he could obtain an annulment and set up a dynasty by a male heir. During this period, each monarch after him determined the state religion.

2.041 Example:
John Wycliffe considered the Bible, not the pope, to be the only true measure of Christian conduct. He and his followers made the first major translation of the Bible into English. Martin Luther believed in salvation through faith and a simplified church service. Calvin believed in the doctrine of the elect. He brought a system of logic and organization to Protestantism.

SELF TEST 1

1.01 f

1.02 j

1.03 b

1.04 i

1.05 a

1.06 c

1.07 e

1.08 h

1.09 d

1.010 g

1.011 system of government intervention to promote national prosperity and to increase the power of the country.

1.012 By custom, coastal towns supplied ships for money in emergencies. Charles I asked for money instead.

1.013 civil conflict in France in 1647 to 1652

1.014 export more than is imported

1.015 a. Habeas Corpus
Either order:
b. Whig Party
c. Tory

1.016 a. Spain
b. Austria

1.017 Spanish Succession

1.018 French and Indian War (Seven Years War)

1.019 England stayed independent and Protestant. England emerged as a sea power.

1.020 Any order:
a. no taxation without parliamentary consent
b. no one can be imprisoned without trial
c. soldiers cannot be quartered in homes in peacetime

1.021 Any order:
a. political—supremacy of King or Parliment
b. religious—national church or religious freedom for Protestants
c. economics—new economic groups wanting role in government.

1.022 French dress and manners were imitated. French became the language of society and many royal courts. Other rulers encouraged the arts and imitated the French court.

1.023 Any order:
a. The more gold and silver it had, the more prosperous a country was.
b. self-sufficiency
c. colonies

1.024 false

1.025 false

1.026 true

1.027 false

1.028 destroy power of Hapsburg and extend France to its natural boundaries.

1.029 once acquired ownership by buying shares which were the wealth of the company. Profits depended on success and share of stocks. If the company failed, one was responsible only for his share.

SELF TEST 2

2.01 a person of Spanish and American Indian descent

2.02 a Spanish province in Latin America

2.03 to sail around

2.04 a policy whereby a certain number of Indian slaves were granted to landowners by the king

2.05 Any order:
a. physical deterioration of the Hapsburg line
b. economic setbacks—no investments in manufacturing or education
c. wars
d. corruption of civil workers

2.06 Any order:
a. lack of resources (money)
b. lack of population
c. lack of size
d. conquered by Spain in 1580

2.07 Hint:
Answer should include the Counter-Reformation, missionizing, educating, and protecting the Indians, and should mention the land ownership and power of the church.

2.08 Hint:
Answer should include the peninsulares, creoles, mestizos, mulattoes, Blacks, and Indians.

2.09 j

2.010 a

2.011 e

2.012 d

2.013 k

2.014 f

2.015 b

2.016 g

2.017 h

2.018 m

2.019 i

2.020 l

2.021 d

2.022 d

2.023 d

2.024 c

2.025 b

2.026 a

2.027 d

2.028 d

2.029 a

2.030 c

2.031 true

2.032 true

2.033 false

2.034 true

2.035 true

2.036 false

2.037 false

2.038 true

2.039 false

2.040 true

2.041 c

2.042 d

2.043 b

2.044 h

2.045 f

2.046 a

2.047 e

SELF TEST 3

3.01 a movement emphasizing intellectual freedom and freedom from prejudice and superstition.

3.02 the shielding from harm or danger of a weak country or people by a stronger one

3.03 to have or get exclusive possession or control

3.04 a Spanish conqueror in North or South America.

3.05 Hint:
Answer should include missionizing, educating, and protecting the Indians, and the importance of the church to the Counter-Reformation and the Thirty Years' War.

3.06 Hint:
Answer should include geographic location, the halting of the Turks, the partition of Poland, and Austria's involvement in the Thirty Years' War.

3.07 Hint:
Answer should include the fact that the Muslims thought victory in battle meant divine favor.

3.08 Hint:
Answer should include the advance of European competition, no more monopolies on commercial agriculture, all exports were agricultural, failure to industrialize, and internal corruption.

3.09 true

3.010 false

3.011 false

3.012 false

3.013 true

3.014 false

3.015 false

3.016 false

3.017 Any order:
- a. Serbs
- b. Greeks
- c. Albanians

3.018
- a. Enlightenment
- b. abolishment of torture
- c. religious tolerance

3.019 Any order:
- a. free passage through the straits
- b. territories along the Black Sea
- c. unrestricted navigational rights on that body of water
  or a protection over Christians living in Muslim territory

3.020 e

3.021 l

3.022 i

3.023 a

3.024 g

3.025 b

3.026 k

3.027 c

3.028 h

3.029 f

3.030 j

3.031 p

3.032 d

3.033 m

3.034 o

3.035 r

3.036 n

SELF TEST 1

1.01 c

1.02 i

1.03 b

1.04 f

1.05 g

1.06 a

1.07 j

1.08 h

1.09 k

1.010 d

1.011 monarchy

1.012 Oliver Cromwell

1.013 Spanish Armada

1.014 Either order:
a. Presbyterians
b. Separatists (Independents or Congregationalists)

1.015 military dictator or Lord Protector

1.016 Either order:
a. Whigs
b. Tories

1.017 Catholic

1.018 William and Mary

1.019 Parliament

1.020 Either order:
a. House of Lords
b. House of Commons

1.021 true

1.022 false

1.023 false

1.024 true

1.025 true

1.026 true

1.027 false

1.028 true

1.029 true

1.030 true

1.031 b

1.032 b

1.033 c

1.034 d

1.035 a

1.036 a

1.037 Either order:
a. The Whigs wanted the real power to be held by Parliament, with a king who was merely a figurehead.
b. The Tories wanted a strong hereditary king with greater power than Parliament, and for the Anglican Church to remain strong against Calvinists.

1.038 a. composed of clergymen and selected nobles, a house of Parliament.
b. composed mainly of middle class citizens; the lawmaking body of England from which the prime minister is chosen.
c. the true head of English government; brings the rulers' ideas to cabinet and Parliament; is the recognized leader of the majority party in the House of Commons.

SELF TEST 2

2.01 the governing, law-making body of Great Britain

2.02 king's belief that it is God's will for him to rule

2.03 Roundhead leader whose direction won victory over the Cavaliers, setting himself up as military dictator after abolishing the monarchy

2.04 acts and laws which interfered, limited, and hindered United States' trade with foreign countries to England's advantage

2.05 one of England's attempts to further tax the United States' colonies by placing tax stamps on various documents

2.06 was the final English victory in the French and Indian War, bringing French surrender and English control of Canada and land east of Mississippi River

2.07 opened up the hostilities and actual fighting between the colonies and England

2.08 gave the desperate Continental army a psychologically-needed win, giving them incentive to keep fighting

2.09 final American victory which brought the British surrender

2.010 an inspirational victory for the United States navy which was greatly outnumbered by British ships

2.011 Parliament

2.012 Calvin

2.013 Either order:
a. Bill of Rights
b. Habeas Corpus Act

2.014 a. Englishmen
b. charters

2.015 a. council to the governor
b. assembly

2.016 mercantilism

2.017 Either order:
a. French
b. English

2.018 Constitution

2.019 Either order:
a. legislative
b. judicial

2.020 Either order:
a. House of Representatives
b. Senate

2.021 false

2.022 true

2.023 true

2.024 false

2.025 true

2.026 true

2.027 false

2.028 true

2.029 false

2.030 true

2.031 Colonies were founded by companies or proprietors. Land was either purchased from the king or given in payment of a debt or favor to the king.

2.032 It gave the colonists valuable training for war and resulted in freedom from French harassment as they moved west.

2.033 a. Advantages—fought on home soil, given psychological edge in protecting homes and geographical edge in knowing the terrain
b. Disadvantages—British were better equipped and organized on land and sea, and congress could not raise taxes to support the war

2.034 <u>England</u>
-Prime Minister
-Parliament
-House of Lords, House of Commons
-Prime Minister and cabinet
-leader of majority party
-when Prime Minister is no longer in majority party, leader of majority party replaces him
-Bill of Rights

America
-President
-Congress
-House of Representatives, Senate
-Executive Branch
-candidate for party receiving most electoral votes
-election every four years
-Bill of Rights (first ten amendments)

SELF TEST 3

3.01 k

3.02 f

3.03 d

3.04 g

3.05 h

3.06 a

3.07 i

3.08 c

3.09 e

3.010 b

3.011 Either order:
a. Whigs
b. Tories

3.012 a. Parliament
b. king

3.013 Either order:
a. Trade acts or laws
b. taxes

3.014 a. Cornwallis
b. Yorktown

3.015 Either order:
a. the nobles
b. middle class and peasants (everyone else)

3.016 Declaration of the Rights of Man

3.017 draft or conscript

3.018 a. First Consul
b. Emperor Napoleon I or Emperor

3.019 Code Napoleon

3.020 Hundred Days War

3.021 false

3.022 false

3.023 false

3.024 true

3.025 true

3.026 false

3.027 false

3.028 true

3.029 true

3.030 false

3.031 c

3.032 a

3.033 d

3.034 a

3.035 b

3.036 Example:
Rising nationalism instilled in other countries caused them to want their freedom from France. The Spanish revolt began this desire for freedom; and Napoleon's invasion of Russia, especially his decision to return to Europe, left his army scattered and weak while other nations rose against him.

3.037 Any four: Examples:
the unpopular wife; the near bankrupt treasury; his rejection of the financial proposals; his inability in making decisions; the people's unrest over poor, indifferent leaders, and the people's growing desire for a voice in government

3.038 Example:
The weak leadership under the Directory led to an even more unstable government. French wars were being lost. The people were afraid of takeover and were insecure. They sought and found strength, military genius, and hope for peace and security in Napoleon.

3.039
a. The English monarchy was abolished and Cromwell ruled as dictator. Parliament was controlled by Roundheads.
b. The firing of shots here between English and Americans began the fighting of the Revolutionary War.
c. The combination of French at sea and colonists on land brought Cornwallis' surrender and United States independence.
d. This defeat of Napoleon by combined European forces led to his rule being taken away and his exile to Elba.
e. This final defeat of Napoleon led to his banishment on St. Helena, no longer able to rise to power.

SELF TEST 1

1.01 d

1.02 b

1.03 j

1.04 a

1.05 f

1.06 g

1.07 l

1.08 c

1.09 e

1.010 h

1.011 Middle Ages

1.012 Either order:
a. discipline
b. specific work duties

1.013 Either order:
a. travel
b. trade

1.014 textile

1.015 Either order:
a. iron
b. coal

1.016 Either order:
a. the directors giving orders
b. workers obeying orders

1.017 stockholders

1.018 common factory workers or assembly line workers

1.019 Either order:
a. steamship
b. steam locomotive

1.020 a. water
b. steam

1.021 false

1.022 true

1.023 false

1.024 true

1.025 true

1.026 true

1.027 false

1.028 false

1.029 true

1.030 true

1.031 d

1.032 b

1.033 c

1.034 c

1.035 a

1.036 England had a sufficient work force, enough natural resources, and enough willing investors in industry.

1.037 a. Production increased in the textile industry with the speedier flying shuttle and spinning jenny. America's cotton gin supplied abundant raw cotton.
b. The iron industry was improved with the developments of coke use, blast furnaces, and lighter steel.

1.038 They were established by capitalists investing money to begin factories. The investors were known as stockholders.

1.039 The steam engine enabled factories to be built away from water sources and ran the factory machines. They also boosted the distribution of goods by quicker transportation methods, like the steamship and steam locomotive. Of course, quicker distribution means higher consumption which in turn allows for increased production.

SELF TEST 2

2.01 true
2.02 true
2.03 false
2.04 true
2.05 false
2.06 false
2.07 true
2.08 true
2.09 true
2.010 true
2.011 e
2.012 g
2.013 b
2.014 f
2.015 i
2.016 l
2.017 c
2.018 h
2.019 k
2.020 j
2.021 d
2.022 m
2.023 n
2.024 Industrial Revolution
2.025 consolidation
2.026 steam
2.027 England
2.028 capital
2.029 New England businessmen
2.030 Erie Canal
2.031 Cumberland Road
2.032 a. industrial
b. agrarian or agricultural
2.033 monopoly
2.034 a
2.035 c
2.036 d
2.037 c
2.038 b
2.039 America possessed an abundant working class, natural resources, and investors willing to risk their capital by backing American industry. Also, America's desire to prove herself to England was a psychological factor.
2.040 Water power was still used to power many factories, steam drove many machines and transportation methods by use of coal or oil, and electricity was used for lighting and power in factories, and for telegraph and telephone communication.
2.041 Corporations lowered unemployment and supplied a larger variety of better quality goods at lower cost per unit. They also gave Americans the opportunity to share the profits by investing.
2.042 Stockholders invested their capital in corporations, giving financial backing in exchange for a share of the profits made, and elected corporation officials.

SELF TEST 3

3.01 c

3.02 f

3.03 e

3.04 k

3.05 d

3.06 b

3.07 g

3.08 a

3.09 j

3.010 i

3.011 l

3.012 n

3.013 m

3.014 true

3.015 false

3.016 true

3.017 false

3.018 true

3.019 true

3.020 true

3.021 false

3.022 true

3.023 false

3.024 false

3.025 true

3.026 true

3.027 steam engine

3.028 communication

3.029 industry

3.030 Communist Manifesto

3.031 economic or political

3.032 factory workers

3.033 a. supply and demand
b. competition

3.034 agricultural revolution

3.035 imported goods

3.036 Middle Ages

3.037 communication

3.038 a

3.039 c

3.040 b

3.041 c

3.042 a

3.043 The many injustices and abuses of the working class by wealthy industrialists who shared little of the wealth they made gave rise to this preaching for the proletariat to overthrow the capitalists.

3.044 Roosevelt enforced earlier antitrust laws and brought publicity against corporation practices, thus gaining more cooperation from them. The Clayton Antitrust Act and Federal Trade Commission also controlled illegal practices.

3.045 It has raised the world's economy, increasing the standard of living to a prosperous level when compared with a century before. It also boosted world trade and made nations dependent upon each other for products and quickened distribution of goods around the world.

3.046 They set the patterns of industry in labor-saving devices, the factory system, and labor laws to protect the worker—patterns which later were vital in setting the patterns of American industry.

SELF TEST 1

1.01 g

1.02 i

1.03 h

1.04 k

1.05 a

1.06 c

1.07 d

1.08 j

1.09 f

1.010 b

1.011 nationalism

1.012 imperialism

1.013 Triple Alliance

1.014 Bolshevik Revolution

1.015 Chateau-Thierry

1.016 Central

1.017 conscription

1.018 military

1.019 *Lusitania*

1.020 Two of the three in any order:
- a. airplanes
- b. poison gas
- c. tanks

1.021 true

1.022 false

1.023 true

1.024 false

1.025 true

1.026 true

1.027 true

1.028 true

1.029 false

1.030 true

1.031 d

1.032 c

1.033 e

1.034 b

1.035 c

1.036
- a. formed by Bismarck to isolate France on the European mainland.
- b. formed to balance European power upset by the Triple Alliance.

1.037
- a. brought Austrian-Serbian relations to a head, leading to Austria's declaration of war on Serbia that sparked war declarations throughout Europe
- b. in violating the Belgian neutrality, the German march greatly influenced England's entrance into the war
- c. ultimately led to America's entrance into the war after reported American deaths on vessels trading with England
- d. eventually led to the takeover of the Russian government by the Bolsheviks who withdrew Russia from the war, allowing Germany to combine its troops in France
- e. the Allied stance here held back the previously successful German drive through France and sparked the Allied drive of 1918

SELF TEST 2

2.01 j
2.02 h
2.03 k
2.04 i
2.05 m
2.06 a
2.07 d
2.08 n
2.09 e
2.010 g
2.011 c
2.012 l
2.013 nationalism
2.014 Young
2.015 totalitarian
2.016 Treaty of Versailles
2.017 imperialism
2.018 Paris
2.019 Fourteen Points
2.020 reparations
2.021 League of Nations
2.022 fascism
2.023 false
2.024 false
2.025 true
2.026 true
2.027 true
2.028 false
2.029 true
2.030 true
2.031 true
2.032 true
2.033 a
2.034 d
2.035 d
2.036 c
2.037 d
2.038 The Treaty of Versailles gave rise to bitter feelings and a crushed German economy. This gave rise to the totalitarian government of Hitler.
2.039 By building up their military forces, they increased industrial production and lowered unemployment.
2.040 He took possession of the Rhineland, Austria, Czechoslovakia, and finally Poland.

SELF TEST 3

3.01 h
3.02 k
3.03 g
3.04 a
3.05 l
3.06 e
3.07 i
3.08 b
3.09 n
3.010 c
3.011 d
3.012 j
3.013 m
3.014 nationalism
3.015 imperialism
3.016 Triple Entente

3.017 Axis

3.018 ratification

3.019 Russian Revolution

3.020 Fourteen Points

3.021 League of Nations

3.022 Treaty of Versailles

3.023 totalitarian

3.024 United Nations

3.025 Manchuria, Formosa and the Pescadores Islands

3.026 San Francisco, 1945

3.027 Atlantic Charter

3.028 true

3.029 true

3.030 false

3.031 true

3.032 false

3.033 true

3.034 true

3.035 true

3.036 true

3.037 false

3.038 true

3.039 false

3.040 c

3.041 a

3.042 c

3.043 b

3.044 c

3.045 b

3.046
a. brought Austrian declaration of war on Serbia which brought on World War I
b. This incident and related incidents forced the United States into World War I.
c. forced America into World War II
d. The charter was the framework on which the United Nations would be built.
e. eventually led to armament races in both world wars, making the nations ripe for war

3.047 The United Nations had the strong support of the United States behind it, while the League of Nations was rejected by the United States. These world peace organizations needed the strength of the big world powers behind them to be effective.

SELF TEST 1

1.01 d

1.02 g

1.03 f

1.04 i

1.05 b

1.06 a

1.07 h

1.08 c

1.09 e

1.010 j

1.011 Bay of Pigs

1.012 Sputnik

1.013 General Assembly

1.014 *Détente*

1.015 Warsaw Pact

1.016 Security Council

1.017 Gulf of Tonkin Resolution

1.018 Solidarity

1.019 Pusan Perimeter

1.020 SALT

1.021 Berlin Wall

1.022 Marshall Plan

1.023 Cuban Missile Crisis

1.024 Berlin Blockade

1.025 NATO

1.026 Communism was not to be allowed to spread. The United States would aid anyone in the world to prevent communism from spreading to their land.

1.027 China

1.028 Czechoslovakia

1.029 Soviet Union

1.030 Afghanistan

1.031 Poland

1.032 Teacher check: Full credit should include:

Fall of Communism in Eastern Europe—
- Gorbachev's reforms and decision not to use force to support communism in the satellites
- Unrest in the satellites
- Specific examples of what happened in at least three of the countries

Korean War—
- Division after World War II
- Invasion and Pusan Perimeter
- Landing at Inchon
- Stalemate on the battlefield and negotiating table
- Truce, no treaty, remained divided

Vietnam War—
- French colonial war
- U.S. support of Diem and opposition of Ho Chi Minh
- Gulf of Tonkin incident and Resolution
- Tet Offensive
- Vietnamization, peace treaty, and U.S. withdrawal
- Communist victory

SELF TEST 2

2.01 Europe

2.02 South America

2.03 Asia

2.04 Africa

2.05 Asia

2.06 Asia

2.07 Australia

2.08 North America

2.09 Europe

2.010 South America

2.011 Volga River

2.012 Mount Kilimanjaro

2.013 Lake Tanganyika

2.014 Nile River

2.015 Mount Everest
2.016 Congo River
2.017 Ural Mountains
2.018 Andes Mountains
2.019 Lake Superior
2.020 Sahara
2.021 Asia
2.022 South America
2.023 North America
2.024 Africa
2.025 Europe
2.026 Asia
2.027 North America
2.028 Australia
2.029 Africa
2.030 Europe
2.031 Isthmus of Panama
2.032 Straight of Gibraltar
2.033 Isthmus of Suez
2.034 Indian Ocean
2.035 Caribbean
2.036 b
2.037 e
2.038 f
2.039 g
2.040 d
2.041 i
2.042 c
2.043 a
2.044 j
2.045 h
2.046 true
2.047 false
2.048 false
2.049 true
2.050 false
2.051 false
2.052 true
2.053 false
2.054 true
2.055 true
2.056 Any three:
China
Vietnam
Cuba
North Korea
2.057 Teacher check: student should give a personal opinion and use facts to support it.

SELF TEST 1

1.01 g
1.02 e
1.03 j
1.04 f
1.05 c
1.06 b
1.07 k
1.08 h
1.09 i
1.010 a
1.011 Vikings
1.012 France
1.013 Alfred
1.014 William the Conqueror
1.015 vassal
1.016 fief
1.017 peasants
1.018 songs
1.019 Either order:
a. Chaucer
b. Dante
1.020 Gothic
1.021 false
1.022 false
1.023 true
1.024 true
1.025 true
1.026 false
1.027 true
1.028 true
1.029 false
1.030 true
1.031 a
1.032 d
1.033 b
1.034 b
1.035 a
1.036 b
1.037 c
1.038 c
1.039 d
1.040 b

SELF TEST 2

2.01 j
2.02 i
2.03 d
2.04 e
2.05 k
2.06 g
2.07 h
2.08 c
2.09 a
2.010 b
2.011 Lollards
2.012 popes
2.013 baptism
2.014 Henry VIII
2.015 Society of Jesus
2.016 Index
2.017 Thirty Years'
2.018 Either order:
a. Henry VIII
b. Elizabeth I
2.019 divine right
2.020 ships
2.021 b
2.022 a
2.023 d

2.024 a
2.025 d
2.026 a
2.027 c
2.028 a
2.029 b
2.030 b
2.031 true
2.032 false
2.033 true
2.034 false
2.035 false
2.036 false
2.037 true
2.038 true
2.039 false
2.040 true

SELF TEST 3

3.01 true
3.02 false
3.03 false
3.04 false
3.05 true
3.06 true
3.07 false
3.08 true
3.09 false
3.010 true
3.011 d
3.012 j
3.013 k
3.014 b
3.015 h
3.016 f
3.017 g
3.018 a
3.019 i
3.020 e
3.021 a
3.022 b
3.023 d
3.024 d
3.025 d
3.026 c
3.027 b
3.028 a
3.029 b
3.030 d
3.031 Articles of Confederation
3.032 Bill of Rights
3.033 Any order:
a. nobles
b. clergy
c. peasants
3.034 Napoleon Bonaparte
3.035 Russia
3.036 Waterloo
3.037 Bible
3.038 Eli Whitney
3.039 steam engine
3.040 capital
3.041 The severe Russian winter drove them back.
3.042 General Assembly
3.043 Poland
3.044 Either order:
a. Europe
b. the Pacific
3.045 Japan bombed Pearl Harbor in a surprise attack.

1. f
2. i
3. k
4. a
5. c
6. e
7. g
8. b
9. h
10. j
11. paper
12. a form of writing
13. stone
14. embalming
15. yes
16. Babel
17. the code of laws
18. with great cruelty
19. Daniel
20. Restoration
21. a
22. b
23. d
24. a
25. b
26. d
27. b
28. a
29. d
30. b
31. false
32. true
33. true
34. true
35. true
36. false
37. false
38. false
39. true
40. true

1. false
2. true
3. true
4. false
5. true
6. true
7. false
8. true
9. true
10. false
11. false
12. true
13. h
14. d
15. l
16. k
17. n
18. a
19. m
20. b
21. e
22. f
23. g
24. j
25. i
26. patricians
27. Paul
28. Mark Antony
29. Remus
30. dynasty
31. Alexander the Great
32. untouchable
33. Buddha
34. God
35. bronze
36. c
37. b
38. a
39. c
40. a
41. b
42. d
43. b
44. c
45. a
46. d
47. Aristotle
48. philosopher-kings
49. one god
50. the prophetess who was referred to as the Oracle of Delphi
51. in Greek mythology, the chief god
52. Example: After his death, there were power struggles and poor leadership. The military gained more control, trade was disturbed, provincial battles were waged, and many mercenaries were hired to staff the armies. There was general political and economical unrest.
53. Monasticism began with hermits, men such as Anthony of Egypt, the third century "Father of Christian Monasticism." St. Basil established the first monasteries in the East. St. Benedict founded the monastery at Monte Cassino and formed the Benedictine rule, the basis of European monastic orders. The centers served as hospitals, farms, or centers of learning.

1. true
2. false
3. true
4. false
5. true
6. true
7. false
8. false
9. b
10. g
11. d
12. i
13. a
14. f
15. c
16. e
17. c
18. a
19. c
20. b
21. a
22. c
23. b
24. b
25. Verdun
26. Do-Nothing-Kings
27. Byzantine
28. 400
29. page
30. icon
31. Asiatic
32. investiture
33. fief
34. Example: The Carolingian Renaissance was the period of time during Charlemagne's reign when schools were established, scholars were sought out to teach, classics were preserved, illuminated manuscripts were produced, and Alcuin was brought from England.
35. The Crusades were Christian military expeditions to the Holy Land and the East to win back the Holy Land from Muslim control.
36. The Germans were too concerned with the conquest of Italy, and the various tribes struggled to enthrone their own emperor.

1. a
2. b
3. d
4. d
5. b
6. c
7. c
8. a
9. b
10. c
11. Flanders
12. the War of the Roses
13. Geneva
14. John Knox
15. Any order:
    a. government
    b. literature and thought
    c. the arts
    d. science
16. Any order:
    a. England
    b. France
    c. Spain
17. the Council of Trent
18. Any order:
    a. Michelangelo
    b. Raphael
    c. da Vinci
19. h
20. a
21. k
22. j
23. b
24. l
25. c
26. d
27. i
28. e
29. f
30. m

1. f
2. j
3. i
4. a
5. c
6. h
7. e
8. d
9. g
10. b
11. k
12. l
13. m
14. n
15. o
16. system of government intervention to promote national prosperity and to increase power of country.
17. By custom, coastal towns gave ships to the navy in an emergency. Charles I asked for money.
18. export more than is imported
19. c
20. g
21. a
22. e
23. h
24. d
25. f
26. j
27. i
28. b
29. d
30. a
31. b
32. c
33. a
34. d
35. a
36. d
37. interrelated
38. trade competition from Europeans
39. Cabeza de Vaca
40. Ferdinand Magellan
41. Spain
42. true
43. false
44. true
45. false
46. false
47. true
48. false

1. h
2. d
3. m
4. a
5. p
6. b
7. j
8. l
9. f
10. c
11. g
12. e
13. k
14. o
15. i
16. Either order:
    a. the House of Lords
    b. the House of Commons
17. Prime Minister
18. Any order:
    a. executive
    b. legislative
    c. judicial
19. Any order:
    a. clergy
    b. nobles
    c. middle and peasant classes (everyone else)
20. Oath of the Tennis Court
21. a
22. c
23. c
24. d
25. b
26. d
27. b
28. a
29. c
30. a
31. false
32. true
33. true
34. false
35. true
36. false
37. true
38. false
39. true
40. true

1. h
2. m
3. f
4. j
5. q
6. k
7. b
8. c
9. d
10. n
11. o
12. g
13. a
14. i
15. e
16. urbanization
17. socialism
18. private business
19. free enterprise
20. capitalism
21. collective bargaining
22. Industrial Revolution
23. consolidation
24. reduced
25. monopoly
26. stockholders
27. true
28. true
29. false
30. true
31. true
32. true
33. true
34. a
35. c
36. b
37. d
38. c
39. a. raised the world's economy to a relatively prosperous level

    b. greatly increased because of mass production bringing greater consumption of goods

    c. new transportation methods made it quicker, cheaper, and more efficient

    d. made trade world-wide, bringing interdependence among nations for each others goods

    e. raised to relatively prosperous level in comparison to earlier times
40. It completely changed his lifestyle from an independent, wholesome life where he was his own boss and had pride in his skills, to a city setting where living and working conditions were very poor and he was dependent for everything, losing his self-worth and pride.

1. i
2. g
3. l
4. j
5. a
6. c
7. d
8. k
9. e
10. f
11. m
12. b
13. Treaty of Versailles
14. imperialism
15. Triple Entente
16. United Nations
17. Axis
18. communism
19. League of Nations
20. nationalism
21. West Berlin
22. totalitarian
23. false
24. true
25. true
26. false
27. true
28. true
29. false
30. true
31. true
32. true
33. d
34. b
35. c
36. c
37. Germany was bitter over the harsh terms of the Treaty of Versailles following World War I. German economic depression called for strong leadership which led to the rise of totalitarian government under Adolf Hitler. Hitler's rearmament of Germany brought about economic recovery and the end of depression. Germany then became aggressive, hoping to win back territories it lost after World War I. It seized land from one country after another, finally invading Poland, which led to war.

1. South America
2. Asia
3. Africa
4. Asia
5. North America
6. Europe
7. Europe
8. Asia
9. North America
10. Africa
11. e
12. f
13. c
14. h
15. i
16. d
17. j
18. a
19. g
20. b
21. b. Sputnik
22. d. ASEAN
23. a. Nile
24. a. repatriation of prisoners
25. d. Security Council
26. c. blockade
27. c. Pakistan
28. b. Afghanistan
29. d. Poland
30. b. Europe
31. c
32. d
33. b
34. g
35. a
36. e
37. i
38. j
39. h
40. f
41. a time of closer relations and negotiations between the superpowers during the Cold War
42. a resolution passed by the Congress that gave the president the authority to expand the American role in the Vietnamese War
43. An attempt by conservative communists to take over the government in 1991 failed. This triggered the collapse of the communist party and the division of the Soviet Union.
44. a. Great Britain
    b. France
45. the many ethnic divisions within my nation; each tribe its own culture, language, and loyalty
46. It was allied with the United States (or neutral), a capitalist democracy, and was generally located on the western side of Europe.
47. Any four:
    Belarus, Bosnia & Herzegovina, Croatia, Czech Republic, Estonia, Kazakhstan, Latvia, Lithuania, Macedonia, Russia, Slovakia, Slovenia, Ukraine, Yugoslavia, Uzebekistan, Turkmenistan, Kyrgyzstan, Tajikistan, Azerbaijan, Armenia, or Georgia
48. Isthmus of Panama
49. Isthmus of Suez
50. Any order:
    a. China
    b. North Korea
    c. Vietnam
    d. Cuba

    also: Laos, Mongolia

51. Any two:
    Canada, United States, Mexico
52. Vietnam or Korea
53. a. United States
    b. Union of Soviet Socialist Republics (Soviet Union)
54. true
55. false
56. false
57. false
58. true
59. false
60. true
61. true
62. false
63. true
64. i
65. a
66. b
67. e
68. d
69. g
70. h
71. c
72. f
73. a

1. b
2. d
3. a
4. c
5. d
6. a
7. b
8. b
9. a
10. c
11. Louis XIV
12. John Cabot
13. Jamestown
14. England
15. Shakespeare
16. sun
17. John Wycliffe
18. Martin Luther
19. Roundheads
20. rebirth
21. false
22. true
23. true
24. false
25. false
26. true
27. true
28. false
29. false
30. true
31. c
32. i
33. a
34. b
35. g
36. h
37. k
38. f
39. j
40. e

1. c
2. i
3. f
4. a
5. k
6. d
7. j
8. b
9. e
10. g
11. false
12. true
13. true
14. false
15. true
16. false
17. false
18. true
19. true
20. true
21. c
22. a
23. b
24. c
25. d
26. b
27. c
28. c
29. a
30. c
31. Zoroaster
32. Any order:
    a. fertility
    b. nature
    c. the heavens
33. Restoration
34. Daniel
35. Babylonian Chronicles
36. obelisks
37. cuneiform
38. lunar
39. hieroglyphics
40. Any order:
    a. aristocracy
    b. middle class
    c. lower classes
41. ka
42. Creation of man

History & Geography 1002 Alternate Test Key

1. m
2. b
3. f
4. a
5. c
6. i
7. e
8. g
9. k
10. n
11. h
12. l
13. d
14. d
15. b
16. a
17. b
18. d
19. c
20. d
21. b
22. b
23. b
24. soldiers
25. Hannibal
26. Caesar or Julius Caesar
27. laws
28. Empire
29. circuses
30. Greek
31. Nero
32. Jesus Christ
33. Jews
34. Maximian
35. true
36. true
37. false
38. false
39. true
40. true
41. false
42. false
43. false
44. true
45. true
46. true
47. true
48. true
49. India or Indo-Aryans
50. They were concerned with how men lived
51. He wanted to be a perpetual dictator.
52. Paul
53. Judas Iscariot

1. a
2. d
3. b
4. h
5. g
6. c
7. f
8. e
9. false
10. true
11. true
12. true
13. false
14. true
15. false
16. true
17. false
18. true
19. b
20. d
21. a
22. c
23. c
24. a
25. c
26. b
27. c
28. a
29. Renaissance
30. Any order:
    a. compensation
    b. trial by ordeal or personal combat
    c. swearing a solemn oath
31. e
32. b
33. a
34. c
35. f
36. d
37. j
38. g
39. k
40. i

History & Geography 1004 Alternate Test Key

1. i
2. b
3. e
4. k
5. a
6. j
7. c
8. f
9. d
10. g
11. c
12. d
13. a
14. c
15. b
16. d
17. b
18. a
19. c
20. d
21. true
22. false
23. true
24. true
25. true
26. false
27. false
28. true
29. true
30. false
31. Any order:
    a. Republic of Venice
    b. Duchy of Milan
    c. Republic of Florence
    d. Papal States
    e. Kingdom of Naples
32. Any order:
    a. Huguenots or French Calvinists
    b. Catholics who wanted Catholicism as the only national religion
    c. Politiques
33. a. Calvin
    b. Catholic
34. Example:
    employed such tactics as spying, torture, and execution against anyone who was suspected of being troublesome to the church
35. Society of Jesus
36. c
37. e
38. h
39. a
40. j
41. f
42. i
43. b
44. g
45. d

1. g
2. d
3. b
4. m
5. k
6. j
7. f
8. e
9. c
10. n
11. a
12. i
13. p
14. h
15. l
16. belief that a king ruled by God's will, and was accountable only to God
17. trading company in which several people owned part interest
18. system by which individuals were granted large tracts of land in the name of the Spanish king along with slaves enough to work it
19. f
20. g
21. h
22. i
23. d
24. j
25. b
26. c
27. e
28. b
29. d
30. a
31. c
32. d
33. b
34. c
35. d
36. a
37. Constantinople
38. the Americas
39. manufactured goods or products
40. raw materials
41. Catholic Church or priests
42. true
43. false
44. true
45. false
46. true
47. true
48. false

1. h
2. f
3. a
4. b
5. j
6. e
7. c
8. i
9. d
10. k
11. Either order:
    a. Roundheads
    b. Whigs
12. Either order:
    a. Parliament
    b. king
13. Either order:
    a. House of Lords
    b. House of Commons
14. Either order:
    a. House of Representatives
    b. Senate
15. Either order:
    a. companies
    b. proprietors
16. Example:
    in giving America valuable training in war tactics for the coming Revolution
17. Either order:
    a. National Convention
    b. Estates General
18. a. first consul
    b. emperor
19. Either order:
    a. education
    b. law
20. Russia

21-26 Examples:

21. showed its growing victory in the conflict for power between itself and the monarch, giving the people a voice in English affairs, and eventually, the rule
22. formal declaration of the American colonies' independence from England
23. the surrender of Cornwallis here brought British defeat and America's independence to rule itself
24. stated the rights of every Frenchman to personal freedoms of speech, press, and worship
25. defeat of Napoleon at the hands of the combined European forces led to his loss of power and exile
26. the final defeat of Napoleon after his return to power, ending in his banishment, never to rise again
27. d
28. b
29. c
30. c

1. h
2. c
3. a
4. b
5. j
6. e
7. f
8. k
9. i
10. g
11. Industrial
12. socialism
13. working class
14. middle class
15. urbanization
16. collective bargaining
17. Agricultural Revolution
18. laissez-faire
19. free enterprise
20. capitalism
21. d
22. d
23. c
24. d
25. c
26. Any order:
    a. work force or labor
    b. natural resources
    c. capital
27. Any order:
    a. labor laws
    b. labor unions
    c. government action

1. g
2. k
3. i
4. m
5. j
6. d
7. f
8. c
9. a
10. l
11. b
12. e
13. Triple
14. a. Europe
    b. MacArthur
15. World War I
16. United States
17. a. Churchill
    b. Roosevelt
18. militaries or armies
19. World War II
20. Woodrow Wilson
21. totalitarian
22. Pearl Harbor
23. true
24. true
25. true
26. true
27. true
28. false
29. false
30. false
31. true
32. false
33. c
34. c
35. b
36. c
37. d
38. Examples:
    a. extreme nationalism; conflicts over imperialism; armament race over military buildup; German aggression with railroad and in Balkans; assassination of Ferdinand
    b. economic depression that led to totalitarian governments that increased their military; aggression by Germany, Italy, and Japan, resulting in the German invasion of Poland
39. Examples:
    a. advocates of a just, lenient peace against advocates of a harsh peace
    b. numerous disagreements between the United States and Russia

1. b
2. c
3. d
4. h
5. f
6. e
7. g
8. i
9. c
10. b
11. Asia
12. Europe
13. Africa
14. South America
15. North America
16. Asia
17. Africa
18. Asia
19. Europe
20. North America
21. Congo
22. Sahara
23. Andes
24. Tigris
25. Everest
26. Nile
27. Himalaya
28. Alps
29. Gobi
30. Amazon

31.–37. (Give partial credit on answers.)

31. The American strategy was to contain communism to places where it already existed and oppose its spread at all costs.
32. Both were limited wars fought by a communist north against a non-communist south. The United States aided the south, while the Soviets and Chinese aided the north.
33. A truce was declared, dividing the country along almost the same line as before the war, but the war was never officially ended.
34. Détente was a "thaw" in the Cold War during the 1970s.
35. The Iron Curtain separated free Europe from communist Europe.
36. The Cold War was a series of confrontations between the U.S. and the U.S.S.R. from World War II until 1991 (or 1989) that never quite escalated to a full war.
37. Cuba was installing nuclear missile bases which were detected by U.S. spy photos. President Kennedy ordered the island blockaded to prevent the missiles from being delivered. The Soviets decided not to try to bring the missiles through the blockade; in return, the U.S. agreed not to invade Cuba.
38. the Isthmus of Panama
39. Any two:
    Belarus, Bosnia & Herzegovina, Croatia, Czech Republic, Estonia, Kazakhstan, Latvia, Lithuania, Macedonia, Russia, Slovakia, Slovenia, Ukraine, Uzebekistan, Turkmenistan, Kyrgyzstan, Tajikistan, Azerbaijan, Armenia, or Georgia.
40. Mao Zedong
41. United Nations
42. Berlin Wall
43. NATO
44. Marshall Plan
45. Any two:
    China, Vietnam, Cuba, North Korea
46. a. Asia b. Australia
47. NAFTA
48. h
49. d
50. j
51. g
52. a
53. c
54. f
55. b
56. i
57. e
58. false
59. true
60. false
61. false
62. true
63. true

1. k
2. d
3. b
4. f
5. h
6. i
7. a
8. c
9. e
10. g
11. b
12. a
13. d
14. a
15. b
16. c
17. a
18. b
19. d
20. c
21. c
22. d
23. a
24. g
25. b
26. f
27. e
28. k
29. h
30. j
31. true
32. false
33. true
34. true
35. false
36. false
37. false
38. true
39. true
40. false
41. Any order:
    a. a calendar
    b. irrigation
    c. written communication
    d. local government
42. absolutism
43. Any order:

    a. Huguenots/French Calvinists
    b. Catholics who wanted Catholicism to be the national religion
    c. Catholics who were primarily interested in politics
44. mercantilism
45. Articles of Confederation